THE PROFIT PLANNER

Everything you need to make money in your business.

Are you here because you want to make a living doing and creating things that you love? Are you tired of being ignored and unprofitable? I get it! You want to make your hustle worthwhile and have your website generate a full-time income with part-time effort. Don't we all? I'm here to let you know that this is totally possible. While we have to be patient when we first start out, we also have to recognize the barriers to our own success. It is my hope that this book will knock down those barriers and teach you the game-changing strategies that have allowed me to make $5K in passive income monthly for the past year. Whether you want to book more clients or sell more products, there are many elements that work together to make your business run like a well-oiled machine. You have all the parts and equipment. This book is the coconut oil that will make that process smooth and easy.

If you have been building a business online lately, you have probably heard that "the money is in the list" and that "you need to have your own product" to make the most money online. These are good pieces of advice to follow, and is true in many cases. But if you've never created your own product before, it may seem impossible to complete this task with so many things to do, to complete, and to set up to create your product.

Fortunately, creating your own product or launching a service doesn't need to be mission impossible. In fact, many people who are equally as talented and even less talented than you have mastered the system of marketing automation and email funnels to sell anything and everything online.

When you have a sales funnel, you:
• Make money on autopilot
• Sell more of the products you already have
• Bring in new subscribers and customers every single day with ZERO extra work

If you've been in business for a while, you can create a sales funnel in a few hours, using content you already have and driving traffic to your already existing products. It doesn't and definitely shouldn't take an eternity to build and put these into place. That's why I created this planner for you. In the first half of this book, you will learn exactly how a sales funnel works and what you need to do to build one. In the second half, you will plan out your next funnel and your day. Once you set up your system, you will be able to sell in a completely automated way without having to promote, hustle, and pitch all the time.

This is *our* book, and I want to serve you as best I can by keeping it updated on the latest and greatest strategies and tools. When it gets updated, you get notified. Pretty cool, right? So what I need from you is to give me feedback along the way. Let me know if any parts are confusing and if you need clarification and examples etc. Don't hesitate to tweet, DM or email me your thoughts. The more you share, the more you benefit.

Now, onto the good stuff. See you on the other side!
Emmelie

CREATING AND SELLING AN IN-DEMAND PRODUCT

Imagine going through a great deal of time and effort to create something that nobody wants to buy. You can probably think back to a time when you launched something so exciting, but when no or few sales come through, you become disillusioned by making money online. You might have even gotten annoyed and called the latest coaching program you took "a scam." Regardless of what the scenario is, no demand will always equal zero sales. Before we start building a funnel, we first need to master creating a product or service around a problem that exists and you can solve.

Pick a Problem You Can Solve

One of the keys to successful online sales is picking a problem you can solve. This might sound simple, but too often, people will create a product they like or are excited about, but not something that is in demand. It usually doesn't solve a problem that is currently in the marketplace or that their audience has. As a result, there is no real demand for that product and thus, no sales.

To have an in-demand product, you need to create a product that solves a problem. If this problem is widespread throughout the industry, and you develop an effective solution for it, people from all across the industry will want to get their hands on your item, setting you up for some nice profits. Thus, it is critical that you find a problem you can solve, and then develop a solution for it - whether it's an eBook with information on a solution, a product that can alleviate the problem, or a service that can solve the problem, etc.

You may be wondering, "How do I identify a problem I can solve?" You will need to do some observation and some research.

Another way to find a problem is to pay attention to what your community and people in your industry talk about. If an issue or problem continues to be brought up by several people over a consistent amount of time, chances are that this is a problem you can build a product around in an effort to resolve or alleviate it. This is a problem that is demanding a solution, and you have the opportunity to provide that solution and make good profits by doing it, plus build your reputation as a problem solver and solution creator.

You should have an audience story for each product or service that you create, and it should speak directly to who your potential customer is and why they need what you're offering. Usually, you are told to outline your target market using demographic information. I encourage you to think outside the basic facts. What race, age, or gender someone is will not tell you nearly as much information as their story: what they are struggling with, what they are frustrated by, and what stops them from achieving their goals. These questions will help you hone into what problem you actually solve for your audience and how you can best serve them when you are outlining your product on future planning pages. They will also come in handy when outlining your sales page.

Audience Story:
- What do they struggle with most?
- What's their challenge right now?
- What do they aspire to be/do?
- What sites/resources do they read?
- How do they receive information?
- How are they currently feeling?
- How do they prefer to be talked to?
- What are they trying to google solutions for?
- What can they afford to spend?
- What bad habits stop them from achieving their goals?

When creating your solution, you need to be very keen on its impact. Is it a vitamin, a painkiller or a cure? Is what you're creating something that will help a pain point be avoided, alleviate the pain point, or cure it all together? Is it tackling the symptoms of the problem or the actual disease? When you are clear on the impact, you can then understand how to frame it and how to sell it.

Package it to sell

When creating a product, especially an eBook, you have to pick a title or name that will sell. Though the common saying "don't judge a book by its cover" is used often in contemporary language, unfortunately, most people WILL judge a book, product, course, or service by its cover. This especially holds true for digital products because people can't get to hold a physical product in their hands to make a decision; thus, they only have the cover, title and sales page to go by. This is why the way you brand your product must be in a way that will entice people to buy it.

The name needs to be descriptive enough to alert interested people as to what content is within your book, yet it should not be so long that it turns off the readers or loses their attention. If you are totally stuck on what to name it and how to package your solution in a way that is compelling, cheat. You don't have to have all the answers; sometimes you can borrow some ideas. Here's what you can do. Go on Amazon.com (and even the country-specific Amazon sites, such as Amazon.co.uk) and browse the bestseller books related to your industry and the specific problem you have identified. See what titles are selling well and modify your title accordingly, using those titles as a blueprint to craft your best title. Note, NEVER take a title word-for-word or even use most of the words so that your title looks like it was copied from another's product, but use a similar structure to craft your own title.

By looking at the popular-selling titles on Amazon and other online bookstores (Barnes & Noble, Google Books, Apple's iBooks via iTunes, etc.), you can learn what people are drawn to when it comes to titles (and graphics as well) and use it as a blueprint for your own offering.

Pick a price point

Pricing can be tricky because it is one of the factors that potential customers consider when purchasing the product. It can be overwhelming trying to put a number on your product that is fair to both you and the customer. I have included some basic formulas that can get you started. These are not universal rules, just some guidelines I share with my clients and use to price my own products and services.

How do I calculate your rate and project fee as a freelancer?

1. Divide your annual salary by 2,080. (If your current role isn't in the industry you want to provide services in, look up a typical salary on Glassdoor or Indeed. Payscale also has a calculator that you can use).
2. Take that number and double it (for taxes and overhead's sake)
3. This is your new hourly rate.
4. For project fees, multiply the amount of hours a project will take you by your hourly rate.

How do I calculate the price of a service?

1. Estimate how long it will take you to deliver a service, including email correspondence. Then multiply that by your new hourly rate.

2. Add on any additional costs for the service from service providers, freelancers, tools, software, fees etc. Aside from your actual time, how much will it cost you to deliver the service?

3. Figure out how much it will cost to break-even, and add to it.

Example: I offer an email funnel writing service that takes 2 hours to complete and will require 1 hour of work from my assistant. It also requires that I use a paid tool to capture my customer's information. I price the service out at $197 based on the following:
- Me: $100 (2 hours at $50 an hour)
- My assistant: $20
- Paid tool: $35
- PayPal Fees and other foolery: $10

The minimum I can charge for this is $165 in order to break even, because that's what it costs me to deliver the service. However, you want to increase your price so you can actually make a profit. Confirm that your price is realistic by researching similar services by people who serve a similar audience to you. What are they charging? Can you compete with their prices?

Whether you are selling a product, service or your time, the formulas above are just to give you an idea about where to start. Once you have identified your starting point, do some market research. Confirm that this is realistic by researching rates in your areas and what other freelancers, coaches, and consultants charge. In many industries, you can find average rates with a quick Google search, but if you're stuck go on freelance websites like UpWork and Fiverr. There, you can get a quick idea of what the price range for your industry or type of work is.

How do I calculate the price of a product?

1. Determine your costs of goods sold: how much does it take to make and ship them? Also include the amount that it costs for the products to get shipped to you, the packaging material, etc. Include all of the costs involved in getting the product to exist.

For example, if I order 20 t-shirts in bulk, and it costs $6 per t-shirt, and $30 to ship the order to me, my costs of goods sold (COGS) is currently at $150 for the 20 shirts. If I then had to purchase 20 bags to ship out orders to my customers at $10 per pack, my COGS is now $160. So each shirt really costs $8 to make, print, and ship. Pricing these at $10 would give me a very low profit margin.

2. Research the market to see what your product already sells for and what your audience is willing to pay. For example, college students are a different market than Wall Street employees. Know your customer and what's a realistic investment.

3. Make sure you price your product at least double what it costs you to make, and never go below a 30% profit margin.

Confirm that this is realistic by researching your competitors' pricing. But remember, with the right brand, pricing could be irrelevant. One word: Yeezys. Those sneakers probably cost $10 cash to make and are sold at an astronomical price compared to the competition. Why? Branding. Kanye West and Adidas aren't selling just a sneaker. They're selling a status symbol.

Now onto the common debate: Should you show your prices on your website? I believe in being straightforward and to the point. If you are giving your customers a hard time with their user experience, they will not pay you. Your prices should be easily visible on your website. Nobody is trying to email you to inquire about pricing, to mail you a check, send smoke signals or read hieroglyphics to pay you. Imagine being super excited to purchase something and then having to wait 2 business days for a price, quote or proposal. During those 2 days, you are giving your potential customers to find another solution - elsewhere.

Make it easy to pay you. I'm not sure who started this trend about hiding prices, but transparency will help you close the sale. From your website to your social media posts, just tell us how much it costs so we can make our decision quickly and have payment buttons available so we can complete the transaction before we change our minds. Remember, you cannot create a passive income system if payments require you to do a phone consultation, send invoices, send proposals, or any other manual work.

Plan Your Entire Product with an Outline

As I mentioned earlier in this book, you need to decide whether you're going to create a book, a coaching program, a membership site, an e-course (i.e. series of emails that dive into a topic or issue in depth), a signature service etc. You need to know your target market well enough to determine which format they prefer, as well as what format will be able to best deliver the information/solution so that the problem is solved or alleviated.

Most overeager entrepreneurs will dive right into creation, then run into issues as they go along because they decide to change something or because they forgot to add something and need to go back and add it, etc. This can cause unforeseen complications and make the process of product creation much more difficult and longer than it needs to be.

A good way to avoid such difficulty is to create an outline of your entire product at the very beginning before you do any work (or have any work done) on it. Create an outline of exactly what your product will have in it, whether it's information in an eBook or email series, what features your coaching program will have, what sections your membership site will have, the deliverables for your service etc.

Take some time at the very beginning to determine exactly what information/features/sections your product will have. You know what will make it a valuable product that will solve or alleviate the problem your target market is having. Thus, you need to ensure that information/features/sections are in there, and you need to ensure it's in an easy-to-use or easy-to-digest manner so your target market will get the most benefit from it.

Making an outline of your product before you begin work on it will help to ensure you remain on track and put in the information/features/sections you wish to put into the product without adding parts that will be seen as "fluff" by your customers. Additionally, if you choose to outsource all or part of the product to others, having an outline will help instruct your team on exactly what needs to be included to ensure your product is completed in a timely fashion and has everything in it that you are expecting to be in it.

Here is what should be included in an outline:
1. Be sure to identify the problem that you are attempting to solve or alleviate.
2. Lay it out in a way to show the seriousness of the issue and why it has to be resolved.
3. Lay out your solution in a step-by-step manner to ensure that people can understand how and why it works and be able to implement it.

Create Your Sales Page

Once you have decided on what type of product you are going to create and have determined how it is going to be created, you're ready to begin writing your sales page and setting up your funnel. Both of these are critical to selling your product effectively; after all, people are not going to buy your product if they are not convinced of its ability to help them.

If you are experienced in copywriting, you can likely write your own sales funnel that accentuates why your product can alleviate or solve the problem that the industry is facing. However, most people are not that proficient in copywriting, so many will either outsource this work as well or use some type of coaching program, software, template, and/or copywriting formula to help them create a sales page.

All of these are viable options in creating your sales letter; you will need to choose what works best for you for your specific project. No matter what you are writing a sales page for, you especially need to focus on the headline; if the headline is weak and doesn't identify why people should pay attention to your offer, they won't read the rest of it, and you will have lost the sale. A headline can make or break your sales page. For the sake of time, the term 'offering' will replace product/service/program/expertise. Know that when I talk about 'offering', it applies to whatever it is you are selling.

Your sale page should touch on these sections:
(Be mindful that the lower the price point, the less sections you need to include. If you are selling a physical product like merchandise, you can use the sections below as a script for a video or content through your website).

- What is the problem that your audience is struggling with? (Audience story)
- How is this problem a pain point in their life?
- What is your proposition? How will you change or improve their situation with your offering?
- Introduce the offering in one strong line.
- Outline the offering
- Share what it costs and how they can purchase.
- Make it clear why they need this NOW and why they can't miss this opportunity. Build up urgency here.
- Introduce yourself and why you are the best person for this.
- Set expectations by letting your reader know who this offering is and is not a good fit for.
- Include frequently asked questions and testimonials.

Writing a Persuasive Sales Page

Once you have your sales page written, you need to go back and make the copy persuasive. 'Copy' is short for 'copywriting'. It refers to any words you use each and every day to communicate and persuade. I know it sounds like a lot. But great copywriting is what sells. All the funnels, landing pages and product paths will be pointless if your copy is whack. Effective copywriting does the following:

- Set you apart.
- Makes people smile, laugh or nod their head.
- Makes them feel understood.
- Lets them know they're in the right place.
- Lets them know they found exactly what they were looking for.
- Gets them thrilled to follow you.

The most common mistake that people make with their copywriting is confusing professional with formal. Newsflash: you can write in a way that sounds like you talk, and gets people to love and buy what you sell. You can be you, boo-boo. Think about it. I'm shady, sassy and straightforward, but you still purchased (and are enjoying) this book, right? I didn't have to write any content that sounded like it came from a member of British Parliament in order for it to be valuable. You can write a copy that's true to your voice, intimate without being inappropriate, and persuasive without being pushy. Trust me, it's possible.

Grabbing Attention

You're going to need to build interest and desire for your product. But I know you're probably thinking: Ok, but, how do I do that? How can I make someone want what I have?"

Well, it all starts with attention and engagement, which are increasingly difficult things to accomplish in today's world. These days, everyone's in a rush, everyone is always busy, and it's increasingly rare to get a chance to just sit down and read a long piece of text. Studies even suggest that the Internet and technology in general is causing symptoms very similar to ADD in a lot of people! So, your first objective is to get people to stop and pay attention. That means you need to write in a manner that is efficient and to the point.

Copywriting Tip #1: Avoid long winded sentences or flamboyant language – aim to get your point across in as few words as possible. Clear and concise is the key.

After you have captured their attention, you want to make sure people don't just leave without getting the full picture. If you take a look at most sales pages, you'll notice that they're very long and narrow, that they utilize lots of long, detailed headers and that they have lots of bold, underlined or red text. The reason for this is that most people will skim through your content anyway – so you need to ensure that they can do so and still get the whole story. Even the headlines alone should give enough information that someone might be interested to buy, while the bold and underlined words will also jump out and grab attention. This way even if people are in a hurry, they're still going to be engaged and persuaded to buy your product.

Selling the Dream

So now they're reading and skimming, what are you going to do with that hard-won attention? The answer is that you need to sell the dream and sell your 'value proposition'. You need to get people dreaming about your offering and wishing they owned it. The objective is to make sure people think in emotional terms. They need to understand how their purchase can make their lives better and why they really need it.

What is a value proposition? Essentially, it means understanding how your product really makes lives better. What is the real value compared to other solutions that might exist? Why do your potential customers even need a solution at all? Why will people buy it?

If your product is about making money, then the dream is power, influence and the resources to avoid the stress of debt, to own their time, leave their job, go on big vacations, and to own a big beautiful house! Of course, you also need to describe the product itself and precisely what it entails – it can't all just be abstract, but that's not the focus. The focus is the benefits, not the features.

I'll give you a simple example. People don't buy a fitness eBook for a good read. They don't even buy a fitness book to get fitter. They buy fitness books because fitness books make them feel good about themselves, to impress women or men and to have confidence and good health. That's the 'dream' and that's the emotion you need to tap into. People don't care how long the book is, how many pages it has, or what are the methods inside of it. They care about how it will make them feel.

Copywriting Tip #2: Start writing with a narrative structure. In other words, make your sales pitch a story about how your offering changed your life or how it can change someone else's. This works well because people find it hard to turn off from stories. This is why we'll binge-watch a whole Netflix show in one sitting. We always want to know how they end.

What is key to understand when trying to master sales, is that people buy based on their emotions, not logic. This is the reason that the whole 'value proposition' concept is so important: if you try and sell based on logic alone then people will often realize they don't really need what you're offering and talk themselves out of it. But if you convince them based on emotion, then they'll feel compelled to buy and will find it hard to resist that temptation. The difference is huge and ultimately leads to a lot more sales.

This is also why it's often a good idea to try and get people to imagine owning your product and to make it seem desirable in its own right: in particular, this means using the right language: words like 'feel' and 'looks' help to really paint a picture and are often used by the likes of Steve Jobs and others when selling products.

Building Trust and Authority

You're selling this dream and showing exactly how you're going to help people get there. But that alone is not enough, because people need to trust you. The next thing you need to do is to build trust and authority. This is partly what your sales funnel has been all about leading up to this. The series of emails that you send your subscribers is to get them to learn more about you, your offering, and why you're credible. It should both build excitement and create trust. What makes you the perfect person to solve their problem?

You can further enhance this effect during your sales pitch. You can help people trust you and remove risk by:
- Using social proof like reviews and testimonials.
- Using money back guarantees and other safety measures that make the buyer feel safe.
- Appealing to stats and statistics – such as studies that backup your claims.
- Appealing to figures of authority and thought leaders in your niche.
- Providing your own credentials.

Do all this and you'll find people are more likely to take that risk and buy from you.

Removing Barriers to Sale

Finally, you need to remove those barriers to sale. One way to do this is by combating the dreaded 'buyers' remorse'. This is the sense of guilt that people can feel after they've bought something. You need to remove this by demonstrating that what you're selling is a good deal, or by convincing them that they might even be making some kind of investment! This latter strategy, of course, works particularly well when you're selling something like an information product (book, course, membership site, masterclass etc.) or a service.

The mind is the root of every action and reaction in our world. What we do physically is merely the manifestation of what's going on in our mind. Our actions are extensions of our thoughts. Even when our actions seem to go against our thoughts, they are in fact driven by our subconscious compulsions. Every action and reaction can be traced back to the human psyche.

Customers, consumers or clients are no different. People decide under the influence of psychological triggers. These psychological triggers can be influenced by many factors. While there are dozens of elements that can influence the psyche of an individual, here are the ten most important psychological triggers that convert leads into customers.

1. Pleasure

Every human being is drawn towards pleasure and is averse to pain. Our minds are wired to protect us from the uncomfortable and the painful. Hence our 'comfort zone'. No one wants to suffer, and everyone wants to have a good time. This desire to be pleasured drives people to buy specific products. As a company, marketing professional or salesperson, you need to present your product or service in a manner that will help the lead to imagine some form of pleasure. The product or service could be anything, right from a foot massager to more data. Affordability will always be a quintessentially influencing factor, but the lead will at least be interested in buying or signing up if pleasure is assured. The worst selling products or the duds in any industry are those that exist without offering any substantial pleasure to its intended customers or users.

In order to be able to motivate someone to buy, you need to know what they are motivated by in the first place. Pleasure is not always physical or emotional or psychological. It varies from person to person. Pleasure needs to be well defined in the context of the product and given the kind of audience you are targeting. Let me break this down for you. Pleasure to someone might be sleeping in late. It's having the freedom to leave their job and own their time. That will motivate them to invest in your offering. Someone who goes to the gym gets pleasure from how they look - the satisfaction of looking in the mirror. So if you own a gym, you're not selling abs, you're selling that pleasure and satisfaction. Smart marketers know how to package their product or service and how to convey the message.

2. The Latest and Greatest

People love new stuff. It doesn't matter what the product is. New clothes, new shoes, a new car, a new house, a new phone, a new laptop, a new set of speakers or it could be a new set of wine glasses. Everything new has a special appeal, especially if it's also an original. The pursuit of the new and original can be explained using the proven fascination with novelty. Studies have proved that exposure or anticipation of novelty items increases the secretion of dopamine in the human brain. Hence, it is a neurological trigger. People are chasing that rush from getting that new thing that everybody can't. It's what keeps sneakerheads on line for hours waiting on Jordans and Apple loyalists camping out for the latest iPhone. Everyone wants a piece of the future.

3. Simplicity

Consumers love, complex craftsmanship, complicated mechanisms and wondrous technology, but they don't want to deal with those firsthand. They want these elements inside the product, which must be simple enough for them to use. Everyone uses a remote transponder key but not many want to know a push button ignition works or what the transponder chip actually is. Any product that appears to be complicated or difficult to use will not influence a potential customer to buy. Every product that is utterly simple to use and has some significant utility will always influence someone to at least consider buying.

Most products aren't simple at all. It is the job of the marketer or the advertiser to simplify the product or at least the messaging. If the customer has to make an effort to understand a product or service, if a lead imagines using the product or service to be time-consuming or requiring a too much work, then they will talk themselves out of buying.

4. Curiosity

There is a part of us that wants predictability, certainty and continuity. Then, there is a part of the mind that craves surprises, wants to explore the unknown, and is waiting to be enticed or intrigued. This curious part of our mind can be easily used to generate traction for your offering. This is not the same as the pursuit of something new or original. It is the longing for something different. While we go about our lives in the most mundane and obviously expected manner, we want to try out something new or have a different experience. Any product that has this intrigue or enticement will easily convert leads into customers. Think about those fad diets or weight loss items like tummy tea or waist trainers. With so many opinions about them, it's easy to become curious on whether or not they work. That curiosity will drive you to buy.

5. FOMO

The key is to get people to act on that emotion while it is there, rather than going away and coming back. To do this, you can introduce scarcity and urgency. That means pointing out that your audience needs to buy right now, or risk missing out entirely. You can do this by making out that you only have a very limited number of products left for sale, or by introducing a limited-time discount. Your visitors will hurry up and decide if they are at all interested in what you're offering and buy right away rather than risk missing out on the opportunity. That way, they'll act on their emotional impulses, rather than leaving and deciding against it!

This is a psychological trigger, but has been diluted in recent years for being used, overused and even abused by most companies. Fear of missing out has always been a driving force and has led to overnight bestsellers, but it works only when used sparingly. Companies keep blasting their subscribers with emails, highlighting limited time specials again and again. If the lead knows that you will keep repeating the same offer or similar promotions time and time again, then it doesn't really create any fear of missing out. You essentially become the boy who cried wolf. You will claim a limited time offer and keep extending it and your audience knows it. You will say you have only '100 seats available' and your audience can see right through it. In order to use FOMO to your advantage, you need to make the offers scarce and factual.

6. Verifiable Proof

Whatever it is that you promote, a lead is likely to believe your claims if there is verifiable proof. Products in action, services being endorsed by people, studies or reviews that support the claims will always instil the trust someone needs to make the final decision. As long as there is an ounce of doubt over the functionality or utility, durability or reasonability of a product or service, a lead will not take the plunge. The verifiable proof can be something as obvious as social media following or mass scale endorsement. This is why you often see screenshots of people's revenue, fast sales by the social media famous, and testimonials from other popular people in an industry. The proof that something works comes from showcasing the results or getting support from someone who's got them.

7. Unity

This can easily be the most important psychological trigger, but the reason we mention it last is because a company needs to master the first six to become a brand with a worthwhile following. Community instils a sense of unity. People come together and feel like a part of a larger group. (Are you familiar with the Beyhive?) Human beings are wired to find a common reason to unite. Cultivating a loyal or committed following is necessary for every company to sustain its success.

There is a reason why millions of people around the world line up to grab the latest iPhone. In addition to the pursuit of the latest and greatest and the quest for pleasure, it is the sense of being a part of the larger group of iPhone users and the fandom that drives the people to put in the effort.

Validate Your Idea

Before you run off and spend days or weeks creating a product or a service, you want to make sure that it is something people want and that your sales page will convert them from a visitor to a customer. This step cannot be skipped! If you find out it's not going to sell, then perfect! You will have avoided wasting time and money and can move on to something else. If you do validate your idea, then you've given yourself a much higher chance of winning and have a good starting point. After you've written your sales page, it's your job to start promoting your product or service directly to a small group of people who are your ideal customer. You want to start getting people to your sales page so you know if it's clear and persuasive and if what you're offering is something they want to buy. You can email them, reach out to them on social media, or even give them a call and explain why you think they're a good fit and why they should participate in your beta version or the mini-service.

Here's How You Validate a Product

If you're:
1. Creating a course, dedicate time to creating the first module.
2. Writing a book, outline it and write the first chapter.
3. Creating an app or software, launch a bare bones beta version.
4. Creating t-shirts or merchandise, create mock-ups *before* you send them to print or use a dropshipper to fulfil initial orders.

Share with some potential customers in your audience and ask them for feedback via a survey or a quick call, and if they would buy it at the actual price you're going to set.

Here's How You Validate a Service

If you're launching a service:
- A) Do it for 3-5 people for free or at a heavily discounted rate.
- B) B) If your service takes a huge amount of time, then only do a portion of the service aka a mini-service.

Launching a beta group or doing a mini-service will help you work out the kinks, get feedback, and compile testimonials.

How it works:

I created a mini-service for my Profit Process service, where I write landing/sales pages, email funnels, social media copy and design graphics for my clients. Before completely setting up the service and creating all the content and graphics to promote it, I first started off by offering just the landing page copy. This was a shorter, less work-intensive version of my actual service that helped me identify if it was something people would buy. I promoted it to a small group of people already on my email list. After I completed the service for 10 people over 2 weeks (each paying $35), I knew that this was an offering people needed and ran with it. I fleshed out the service, created a marketing plan, and upped the price to $197.

In order to protect your time and your efforts, these are the steps that you need to take to ensure that you aren't solving the wrong problem for your audience. After you have validated your idea, you can open a wait-list or pre-sale and charge a special price (maybe an early bird price) for your product or service. You can promote this while you finish fleshing out the service or completing the product, and creating your launch/promotion content.

Before I wrote a single word of this book, I created a landing page and started pre-selling based on the templates that will be included in the planner section. I gave a sneak peek on my Instagram story and posted it twice on my Instagram profile. I created a waitlist and offered a special early bird price at 50% off. Once 4 people purchased at the early bird price in 48 hours, and I got over 20 people on the waitlist, I verified this was something that would sell and I started writing.

Let's be clear. "I would buy this" and "Here is my money" are two very different forms of commitment; you don't want to end up disappointed when an "I would buy this" from 1000 people turns into 5 sales when you launch. This happened to me a few days ago, actually. I posted a picture of my new phone case and was flooded with a bunch of comments from women saying they wanted to buy it, asking where they could get it, and how they could get their hands on the case. About 15 comments and 5 DMs about the case turned into two sales. Luckily, I hadn't invested in any inventory and was using a dropshipping service instead. Anyone who doesn't know how to validate an idea would have gotten hype by the interest and ordered a ton of cases in bulk. Interest doesn't always translate to investments. Had I not validated the product, I would have been sitting on inventory because the expressed interest didn't convert into actual sales.

Now, this isn't always necessary for smaller ticket items or things that don't require a massive amount of work, but for large software projects, when you will be investing a large amount in inventory, or launching a new service or business in general this is key.

Create Your Offering

After you have validated your offering, start to build/make/create it and set a launch date. Don't get overly ambitious and rush this process. Give yourself *at least* 4 weeks to complete all the content necessary to properly promote your offering, as well as create the actual offering. You want to give yourself time to write the book, record the videos for the course, flesh out your signature service, and all the other logistics involved in creating something new. If you choose not to listen, get overwhelmed, half-ass it, and it flops, please return to this page, and remind yourself of what I told you.

Create Your Funnel and Product Path

Before we go any further, it would perhaps be useful to explain exactly what a sales funnel is and what you'll be using it for. In essence, a sales funnel can be imagined like a strainer for customers. You start out with a mix of different kinds of people who are on your site and social channels. With a funnel, you narrow those visitors down to include only the most engaged and interested prospects. All the while, you'll be building trust, building engagement and getting them ready to make a sale.

In real life, what this means is a series of different marketing strategies that work together to achieve one goal: make the sale. So you might start with a simple Instagram post, or a blog post, and then get potential interested people onto an email list. After that, you continue to see how interested they are by offering them more information like a free report, then a webinar, then a small product sale, and then a larger investment.

Each of these marketing stages gets you closer to your ideal customer and the sale. Each time a prospect clicks on the next link, or follows you to the next step, they are becoming more and more likely to buy from you. But there is one thing that you can't ignore and keep as the focal point: your email list.

The most important part of any sales funnel is your email list. Without it, you're basically renting eyes on the Internet and are at the mercy of algorithms. If Instagram shut down tomorrow, how would you communicate with your audience? If you no longer had a Facebook page, would your audience be able to find you online?

You're taking a huge risk if you're investing more time on growing your social media than your email list. Followers don't always become customers, but email subscribers give you a whole new opportunity to close the deal.

It's been established that most people require about five points of contact with an online vendor before they'll make a purchase. Sometimes that's because they're shopping around for the best deal or unsure if what you're offering is going to meet their needs. Other times, and most often, it's because they aren't sure they can trust you.

Your mailing list enables you to keep in regular contact with both prospects (people who haven't purchased) and customers. In fact, you'll need a different list for each stage of your sales funnel so you can send more expensive offers to customers (upsell) or send a series of persuasive emails to prospects (nurture funnel).

Now, a funnel is not to be confused with a product path. A product path is a collection of all the pieces of content and interactions that lead your website visitors to purchase. It's the different ways that people find out about your product or service. A sample product path for my Squad Goals Challenge would look like this.

A blog post, sidebar image, welcome bar, Periscope broadcast or tweet, leads my audience to download a social media worksheet. That worksheet triggers an email funnel where the visitor will be educated on the importance of social media for building a brand. Throughout the series, there will be mention of my Squad Goals challenge and a link to the landing page. The blog post, periscope and tweets etc. may also have a link to the landing page as well. The goal of all this free content is to showcase that I'm an expert and get them to the paid offer. The product path gives people multiple opportunities to discover what you're selling, but there is a method to the madness.

Your funnel will take people from free content to a freebie, funnel, or paid offering. This is what a typical product path and funnel looks like:
- Someone finds your website by Googling a problem OR a Facebook Ad.
- They stumble across a blog post that you wrote on the topic.
- They then submit their email address to download a freebie that you're offering like a worksheet, a guide, or a free webinar.
- They are immediately shown a Thank You page with a one-time offer called a tripwire.
- After receiving their freebie, a series of emails are triggered to showcase your credibility and provide a solution to the problem they have been trying to solve.
- Prospect receives 3-7 emails that is trying to persuade them to invest in your core offering or signature service. This is an upsell.
- If the prospect doesn't invest in your upsell, they get a lower priced, less impactful version of your offering called a downsell.

The idea behind building your sales funnel is that research shows consumers are more willing to purchase a cross-sell or upsell offer at the same time they purchase an item. A cross-sell example is when someone orders a burger at a fast food restaurant and then orders fries and a soft drink at the same time. An upsell example is when you buy a tool and then buy the accessories with it to make it a more powerful and/or useful tool. The same concepts apply to Internet marketing, which is why having a sales funnel is essential to maximizing your sales and profits.

Creating a sales funnel means that the prospect will be introduced to various offerings at different price points. You must plan out your sales funnel carefully based upon what you have to offer to your target market to alleviate or solve their problem so that you can maximize your sales and profits. This will require a tripwire and a downsell in addition to your core offer. Let's walk through this.

Your Freebie Aka Opt-in

The goal of your freebie is to build your email list with people who are interested in what you're selling. It's not simply about being nice, it's about being strategic and broadening the amount of people who know that you exist and are introduced to your offering. An email list is valuable for so many reasons. It is a database for your customers that you take with you regardless of what social media platform is popular, what your website domain is, or the industry you are in. In addition to creating this permanent database of customers, an email list is also important for marketing and sales. There is no guarantee that your entire audience will see your post on any given social media platform. With email however, at least you know that your message will hit inboxes. Whether they open it or not, is a story for another day.

The reality is: "Sign up for my newsletter" and "Stay updated on my blogposts" is not enticing enough to drastically grow your email list. C'mon. 1 or 2 subscribers at a time is not going to explode your business. The fastest way to exponentially grow your email list is to be valuable. You have to provide value and begin to solve their problem.

You need to send them lots of information to prove that you actually know what you're talking about and that they won't be wasting their time and money buying from you. You also need to make sure people remember who you are and what you do. You know the old expression: Out of sight, out of mind. People can sign up for your email list, but if you don't work on building that relationship quickly, they will forget who you are and unsubscribe. You need to offer real VALUE here. The freebie that you offer should be something you could easily sell for money, but instead, you're giving it away for free.

Before you sit here and tell me that you already have a freebie or an opt-in, ask yourself: Do I have a generic freebie, or a highly targeted and specific one for the product/service I'm trying to sell?

This is the mistake that the vast majority of business owners are making right now. They try and sell an audience who isn't necessarily interested in what they are selling. They aren't primed for the sale. This is why your freebie is soooooooo important. If the right people aren't in the funnel, they will never ever buy.

The key is to answer the questions and provide the solutions that directly relate to what you are selling. For example, just because people ask a lot about advertising when it comes to marketing, that's not something to create a freebie around because none of my products or services relate to that. It's important to stay in your lane so that you attract the right people to your email funnel.

How do you know what to give away? Find out what people are asking about already.

1. Look at social media comments - your own, your competitors, and your peers. You'll find the same questions keep popping up over and over again.

2. Browse through forums like Yahoo! Answers and Quora, where people post questions for others to answer. Here you can identify what people are stuck on or what they need to know. Jot down any trends that you notice.

3. Harness the power of search. Visit sites like Soolve, YouTube and Google and type in your industry or topic and see what people are already searching for and what people need answers for.

4. Look at your analytics and see what your most popular post is traffic wise. Then, go on BuzzSumo and see what your most popular content is based on social media shares. You should see some overlap happening between traffic and social. Choose a topic that is already popular and relates directly to what you are selling. You don't need to reinvent the wheel.

You should never go into your freebie blind. The same way that you validate your product or service before launching, you should also validate your content. You should know what your audience is in need of, but if you don't the suggestions above will get you on track.

Once you have your freebie, you need to make sure people know about it. The freebie would be added and mentioned on related blog posts, videos, or audio content that you create or have created. The easiest and one of the most effective is a free email course that drives people into your paid product with strategic and intentional marketing messages and pitching. You educate them then excite them. New visitors move through your funnel, get introduced to you and your product, and are educated, given tons of value and pitched strategically throughout.

An opt-in product can also be a worksheet, eBook, email course, freebie, virtual conference or other digital product or offering that you give away for free in exchange for someone's email. While there are a ton of options out there for you to choose from, I'm going to give you the answer: start with a 3 or 5-day email course. Here's why:

1. Minimum graphic design necessary.
Aside from the header that you need to design (on Canva preferably) to make your emails look cohesive, the rest of the work is writing the text. You don't need to worry about layout, fonts, colors, or pdfs. All you need to do is write.

2. Less creation time.
You can launch immediately after you write the first 2 days. You don't need to wait until the entire course is done to begin promoting it and have people sign up. You can easily continue adding to the course while it is running.

3. More perceived value.

A worksheet or a 5-day course? It's a no-brainer. The course is going to seem more valuable, because it is a guided experience and has more content. However, there may be some drop off in your course. A lot of people aren't very consistent and won't make it all the way through. Don't take it personal. Your job is to deliver the course and collect their emails.

Let's get to it. Here is how you can create your first email course and have it ready to go tomorrow by the time you're watching Insecure.

1. Pick a topic.
Your topic needs to address the needs of your audience. What are the questions that you are constantly asked? What does your audience want to know most about? If you're smart, your email course will be a preview to another product or service. Got it? Great!

2. Name the course + design the header
Now that you have your topic in mind, name your course and design your header on Canva. They make it easy to size headers for email. They even have templates for you to use.

Name your course something catchy that speaks to the outcome of the course. If you are like me and love alliteration, make sure to have a subtitle to give some details. It might be The Single Girl's Guide to Dating in Atlanta or Date Better: A 5 Day Course to the Best Date Spots in Atlanta. Whatever title you choose make sure that it is enticing and will make people think: "I have to sign up to get this information!"

3. Outline the 5 days
Now that you have some direction, jot down what you will talk about each day. Do not overthink this. Walk them through how to do something or share one new point each day. For example, this email could be an email course. I could have broken down each step into a day and gotten really in-depth. However, I chose to share a new point each day, so you will be getting different tips all related to the topic of creating passive income and building a better website.

4. Set everything up in your preferred email provider.
If you're just getting started, Mailchimp is a good option. It's usually free until you pass 2000 subscribers. Once you create your Mailchimp account, you will set up your emails in the Automation section in the header. If you can afford it, try Convertkit, which is more robust and easier to use in my opinion.

5. Nail the copy.
Your subject lines will make or break your course. Use the Headline Analyzer on CoSchedule to help you write better subjects and titles. Again, make sure these are results-oriented so people are compelled to open. Once you have the subject, get to writing the meat of it. Think of it as a blog post in email form. Show people how to do

something by including videos, links to other resources, and other extras that will boost the value of the content.

Your Tripwire and Downsell

After someone downloads your freebie or signs up for your course, they should see a tripwire. A tripwire is an affordable limited time offer that is valuable and aligns with the freebie they just downloaded and the item you are trying to sell. This is shown on the thank you page after someone downloads or signs up for your free item and is typically priced under $47.

This is where you make an amazing offer that they will see only ONCE, ever. It's a super limited time, one time only, get it now or lose it forever kind of deal. The value should be through the roof and it's got to be worth far, far more than the asking price. As an example, this is a great place to offer a best selling $97 product for $9.99.

An alternative is to offer a $1 trial into a membership. If you can also offer a lower monthly rate on a high priced membership, or if the membership is in the $7-$20 a month category, you should do great.

Remember, you want to promote something on the Thank You Page because this is where you want to break even. That is, if you're buying advertising like Facebook Ads or Instagram shoutouts, you want the profits from your Thank You Page to PAY for your advertising, so everything else you make in your funnels is pure profit.

In addition to a tripwire, you're also going to need a downsell option. A downsell is another affordable limited time offer presented to the potential buyer *after* they miss or pass on the core offering. Perhaps they weren't ready to buy, missed the deadline, or didn't want to make a large investment. Increase your chances of making a sale and helping them solve their problem by having something you can downsell them on. This could be your mini-service or a product with less features.

Service Example:

Let's say you are a relationship coach. When creating content, you decided your freebie was going to be an eBook: 10 Tips to Take You From Single to Engaged. The Tripwire is a $9 eBook or training video on how to be more successful at dating in your 30s. An upsell to the core offering would be a $149 hour-long coaching session to creating your Dating Success Map. If the prospect passes up that offer, you can downsell them to a $75 half-hour "Pick my Brain" session.

Product Example:

You own a t-shirt line and you want to build your email list by offering a 20% off coupon as a freebie. Once they submit their email for the coupon, your prospect will see a tripwire for free shipping if they purchase within the next 15 minutes. The upsell would be to get them to purchase your core offering which is a 3-t-shirt bundle. If they don't bite, you can offer them the downsell or a buy one, get one free offer.

A Digital Product Example:

You want to sell a $397 online course. You offer a freebie to get interested people on your email list, a free webinar with no replay. The tripwire is $27 for lifetime access to the webinar recording and accompanying worksheets, so they can start to begin to solve their problem. The upsell is the $397 course with an additional planner and templates. If they do not invest in the course, you can downsell them the planner and the templates instead.

Then it's time to write the emails.

Your Email Sequence

So what's a funnel? An email funnel is simply a series of emails and content that guides your new email subscriber from reader to customer. A funnel can be made up of webinars, resources, emails, video content, or any other kind of content that you feel comfortable producing.

ATTRACT

1. The Before + After
Explain why your audience needs this particular product or service. Why it is important to you, and how it has affected you and your life. This should be a before and after where you show your audience where you were and that you understand their struggle, then you follow-up with where you are now.

Product Example: How Eyelash Extensions Saved My Mornings.
Service Example: The Tool That Allows Me to Make Money While on Vacation.

2. The Why
Share 3-5 reasons on how your audience live, work, and career etc. will change if they implement or buy your product or service. Why do they need to buy this? Why do they need to buy it now?

Product Example: Why You Need to Get Eyelash Extensions This Summer Service.
Example: 3 Reasons You Need Funnels in Your Business.

CONVINCE

3. The Preview
Show your audience how to do something. You want to show them the beginning, middle or end of what you are selling with a how-to, tutorial or training. You want to give them a glimpse into what they will be getting, so they can get excited about the rest.

Product Example: How to Care for Your Eyelash Extensions Service.
Example: How to set up your email funnels in Mailchimp.

4. 3-5 Biggest Mistakes or Myths
This is a marketing message where you will present your product or service as a solution to your audience's problems. You will bust myths or address misconceptions that may be stopping them from purchasing your product.

Product Example: 3 Mistakes Women Make When Choosing a Lash Artist Service.
Example: 5 Myths Newbies Believe About Creating Passive Income.

CONVERT

5. Behind-the-Scenes
Nothing gets people more hooked than something they can't have. Entice your potential customers by giving them a sneak peek into what they can expect once they purchase. This is a good place to include mock-ups, explainer videos, customer stories, and other collateral materials that will help you sell your product.

Product Example: How Lash Extensions Help Your Natural Lashes Grow Service.
Example: Maria's Secret to Making $2K Monthly.

6. The Sell
This email is the final email and pitch you will send your audience. It will be straightforward and to the point where you will ask them to buy your product. You will clearly outline the product or service as if the email was a mini landing page. You will also answer any questions or address any doubts they might have about the purchase. Finally, you will include testimonials and a few more facts, photos, and content that prove that what you sell is worth the investme
Product Example: What's Holding You Back From Investing in Your Transformation?
Service Example: The Answers to Email Funnels You've Been Waiting For.

This sequence can be as long or as short as you want, as long as you focus on attracting, convincing and converting. It can take the form of a full email funnel or can be a product path that encompasses a set of emails, blog posts, webinars and other content. It's up to you how you want to divide it.

Create Content to Promote Your Freebie and Your Offering

Identify all the pieces of content that relate to a particular product or service, and ensure that the freebie and the product or service's landing page is linked throughout. In addition to upgrading content you already have, you should create at least 2 blog posts/videos/podcasts on the topic that you are offering a solution for, and at least one freebie/opt-in to collect emails and build your list. Remember, freebies can be eBooks, worksheets, email challenges, quizzes, or short webinars. You will offer them the free resource in exchange for their email address.

The content you create should always speak to the current problem that they are having in their lives. What are they struggling with? What is the root cause of the struggle? Once you have these answered, speak to that.

Make sure that all your content is directly related to the reason why they signed up in the first place. Share tips that will help them solve their problem or help them move their passion forward. The more helpful you are with your information, the longer they'll read your emails and buy your products.

Service Example

Struggle: Single
Root Cause: Looks, Bad Conversation Skills, Bad Sex, Too Thirsty, Self-Esteem etc.

For example, if I am an author selling a book on how to find your future husband, this is some content I would create:

Blog Post: Why you're still single after so long.
Video: How to prepare to find your future husband.
Freebie: 10 Tips to Take You from Single to Engaged eBook.

Product Example

Struggle: Foodie lacking community.
Root Cause: No way to be united with other foodies or being able to easily identify them.

For example, if I am selling merchandise like pins, hats, and shirts for foodies, this is some content I would create:

Blog Post: 10 Best Places to Find Foodie Friends.
Instagram Live: 10 Ways to Wear Pins This Summer.
Freebie: 20% off Discount Code.

Track Everything

Google Analytics, also commonly referred to as GA, is one of the many services offered by the search engine giant Google. The tool records every activity to, on and from your website, which helps you know exactly how your website is performing. GA records the traffic to a website, the redirected or rerouted visitors from other sites, search engines, directories, advertising platforms or even people accessing a website by directly entering the URL onto a browser. The tool goes even further and records the amount of time a visitor spends on a website or on a given webpage within a website, the geographical location of the user or viewer, whether or not the user is eventually buying anything, signing up for a service or expressing interest in a product. Right from the advertisement links to referring through social networks, every source, route and access of a user is recorded. It records every piece of data in real time and offers a quick real-time snapshot.

Setting up Google Analytics

Setting up your Google Analytics account is very simple, and the entire process can be done in a few minutes. The first thing you need is a general Gmail account. Once you have a general Google account, you should go onto the Google Analytics page where you will be asked a few simple questions. After you complete the sign up process, you will get a tracking code from Google Analytics. This tracking code needs to be inserted in your website for Google to start recording data. You can do so with a Wordpress plugin or on your specific provider. GA does a great job of walking you through your specific provider.

Once the code is in place, it will begin collecting data and you can login to your Google Analytics account and start observing the analysis in real time on the dashboard. What I want you to focus on now is tracking the links for your campaign. UTM Tags in Google Analytics will change your life. They are specific labels that tell your analytics where your traffic came from. If your Google Analytics aren't set up properly, stop everything you are doing and slide over to Fiverr and get a freelancer to get it done. After you've done that, you are going to want to outline a few things as you prepare to get these UTM tags together.

1. Name your campaign.
2. Outline the sources where the traffic to your pages will come from: Social Media, Google, Ads, Website, Email Etc.
3. Decide what the mediums are going to be specifically.

Examples:

Source: Social Media // Medium: Instagram, Twitter, Facebook Page.
Source: Ads // Medium: Influencer A Profile.
Source: Website // Medium: Sidebar or Footer or Blogpost.

Source: Email // Medium: Newsletter or Funnel Email.

4. List all the specific content if you want to compare even further.

Example:

Source: Website.
Medium: Blogpost.
Content: Topic A.

Source: Email.
Medium: Funnel Email.
Content: 2nd Email.

After you have all of that outlined for every piece of content you want to track on your campaign, now you have to build the links here: **https://ga-dev-tools.appspot.com/campaign-url-builder/** (It's probably easier to just search "Google Analytics Campaign URL builder").

Create links for the sales page and your freebie page. You want to know how people got on your list and how people ended up purchasing. After you plug in all the info, you shorten the links and use them to promote your content. These links will be used instead of the normal URLs you would use. For example, if you were promoting on Twitter, you would use the URL that you created with Twitter as the medium. If you are inserting the link to your sales page in an email, you will use the URL where you indicated that email was the source.

This can be a time-consuming process if you've never done it before, so that's why it is important to give you enough time to not only launch, but also create all the pieces necessary to track.

LAUNCH!

After you have planned out and created your funnel, your product, and your content, it's time to set the plan in motion. You should have your blog posts proofread and scheduled, your emails loaded, and your sales pages up and running. It is best to have all of the moving pieces in place before you hit "play" on your campaign. Forgetting one small detail can throw everything off, and you will have done all that work in vain. Once you have tested everything and verified that your funnel works and runs smoothly, you're officially ready to launch.

Set Your Sales Goal

Whether you're striving for $5K or $50K a month, being successful in business is simple math. But we're so obsessed with building six-figure businesses that we get overwhelmed with self-doubt. We keep failing because we're running before we know how to crawl. We want to say that we have a six-figure business, but we've been avoiding the hard work. Striving for five-figure launches and months, and haven't figured out how to make $500 a week. There's a disconnect.

So many entrepreneurs don't know their profit margins, cost of goods sold, or their best-performing channels (Instagram, YouTube, Website etc.), which are crucial to making good marketing decisions. Once I mastered the numbers game of sales and revenue, I was able to master the marketing side of it. You see, we spend so much time worrying about social media posts, blog posts, email funnels, and sales pages, that we forget to get down to the basics: having a plan. The goal alone isn't enough. Instead of worrying about building a six-figure business, let's figure out how to make $100 or $200 dollars a day. (I actually created a business calculator to help you figure that out).

$100,000 seems like an overwhelming number, but setting bite-sized goals helps. If you want to cross into the illustrious six-figure club, you need to make $275 dollars a day. Not too bad right? When you break down that large revenue goal into a more digestible one, you can breathe a sigh of relief because now it feels doable. Once you have your daily revenue goal, it's time to map out what that looks like in real life.

This is how you hit that revenue goal.
The first thing you need to do is break down daily revenue goal into actual product goals.
1. Decide how much you want to make per month from your offering.
2. Divide that monthly revenue number by the price of your offering. This will give you the number of sales you need to make to hit your revenue goal.
3. Divide that sales goal by 30 or 31 (depending on the month) and it will tell you how many sales you need to make per day.

Getting New People into Your Funnel

This is where you create a cadence for releasing the content you just spent a month working on. You can spend anywhere from 2-6 weeks 'launching' an offering depending on the price point. The term 'launch' refers to a specific amount of time that you are dedicating to promoting a specific offering. I recommend at least 4 weeks. Your schedule will look a little something like this:

Day 1-14: Capture Leads for Your Email Funnel

This is where you see who is interested in your offering. Your goal is to build an email list of potential buyers who have the problem you are trying to solve for them. These are the things that should be happening at the beginning of your launch.

- Publish and promote your blog/podcast/video and freebie.
- When someone signs up for your freebie, they should be redirected to your page with the tripwire and upsell options. (Opportunity for more $).
- Send out an email to your already existing email list about your new offering and the 'resources' (aka the content you created) around the service.
- Start promoting on social media daily.

Day 15-30: Sell, Sell, Sell.

This is where you drop your other pieces of content and any premium freebie like an email challenge, quiz, or free webinar etc. Your goal is to seize every opportunity to pitch to your audience. You will focus on the hard sell, creating urgency and getting sales. You would also trigger your email funnel to start running to the new list you started building on days 1-14. If your funnel is written properly and your sales page is persuasive, you should see the sales starting to roll in.

When you launch your campaign, start doing some outreach to get some fresh eyes on your content and increase your visibility. This is where public relations and guest posting becomes important. Being featured in the press or on someone else's site will get you a whole new audience. Strive to land a guest post, podcast interview, video interview, or another kind of media placement at least once of these a week when you're launching. This is also a good time to book speaking engagements.

Eventually, you will max out the promotion of your offering to your current audience. This makes is critical that you find new eyes for your content and sales page. This is where amplification comes in. Think: how can I amplify this outside of my network? These are the things that you should be focusing on during the second half of your launch:

- Send product to Influencers or celebrities.
- Partner with a similar company on a giveaway or a promotion.
- Run FB ads or IG ads.
- Get affiliates on-board.
- Land at least 2 sponsored posts or interviews to promote your offering.
- Invest in Instagram Takeovers or sponsored posts from influencers.

Getting Traffic

It's important to realize that there is no free traffic. You're either paying for traffic with your time or with your money. And the sooner you can pay for it with your money, the better, because then you can begin growing your business at a much faster pace.

Regardless of whether you're paying by time or by money, there are smart ways and some silly ways of getting traffic. Initially, it can be very frustrating to try to create traffic streams yourself. For example, starting a blog and trying to get people to the blog so you can get them to your squeeze page is hard work and takes time. It's worth the investment, but realize it probably won't pay off for six months or more. That's why when you're first starting out, you want to find traffic streams that are already in place and tap into those like Facebook ads and Instagram ads.

For free traffic, social media is your #1 channel. Post often and everywhere. Post great content and be helpful. If you can, partner up with other people who have lists and work out deals. Offer to pay them to put a banner on their site or to recommend you to their readers. Guest blog, and at the end of your posts offer readers you free gift. Do ad swaps with other list owners and website owners. Offer to pay a flat rate to large list owners if they'll offer your free gift to their subscribers. The scope of traffic possibilities is much larger than we have room to cover here, so do some research and find the 2-4 methods that resonate with you and your offer.

And keep in mind that once you have your funnel set up, you can devote nearly all of your time to getting traffic because everything else runs on autopilot. This means once you can afford to BUY your traffic, this will become practically a hands-off business, and you can invest your time setting up a second and a third funnel, and so forth.

Measure and Analyze

As you are launching and promoting, you want to be sure that you are keeping track of two things: what's working and what's not. Adjust after the first two weeks and focus your efforts on the channel that is working the best.

Have you made more sales on Instagram? Go heavy with the ads here.
Was your video viewed more than your blog posts? Do another video instead of blogging.
Is there a tweet that is performing better than others? Boost it.

Double down on what is working well and pull resources away from the things that are not. You can easily figure out what is working well by looking in your Google analytics dashboard. All you have to do is go to the 'Acquisition Menu' on the left-hand side then click 'Source/Medium'. This will only work however if you took the time to create your URLs with UTM tags.

THE PLAYBOOK
Strategies to Get More People on Your Email List and in Funnels

FREEBIES

In order to consistently grow your list, you have to continue to give people new content they can sign up for. This is where the other digital content I mentioned comes into play: worksheets, eBooks, checklists, virtual conference, Periscopes, podcasts etc. Growing your email list is ABC: Always Be Collecting. Give people so many options to join your list that there is no possible way they can leave your site without it. Your job is to think about what already existing content do you have that you can package into a freebie. Have a couple Periscope videos that you can group together into a course? Have a worksheet or video tutorial that you can create to help people learn something easier? Have an extremely long blog post that you can make into a short PDF guide? Be mindful, you need to create a new signup form for each freebie and ensure that you set up your email provider to deliver the freebie upon sign-up.

Action Item: Identify and create at least two new freebies that you can create based on your top five best performing blog posts, videos or other content.

POPUPS

We have all been held hostage by a pop up. You know. You're ready to leave a webpage and boom, a pop up appears asking you to sign up for the newsletter. Luckily for you, you aren't going to be corny and just ask people to sign up to your newsletter that may or may not be valuable to their life. You are going to invite them to download this amazing freebie you created or enrol in the course to answer the question that led them to your site in the first place. You can set the pop-up to appear after a certain amount of time (30 seconds) or on exit intent (when they are about to close out of your site.) I recommend going with exit intent, because you may set the pop up to appear too early and disturb the reader or too late and they are already gone.

If you have Wordpress.org, Popup Ally is the best plugin to create pop-ups for your site. If you have Squarespace, you can use SumoMe.

Action Item: Create a pop-up for your freebie. Remember, the resource you choose should be valuable to all your visitors.

END CONTENT

Your blog is probably the most visited area of your website because it constantly has new content for you to share. While a blog is NOT, I repeat, is NOT necessary for every website, it is a common way to increase traffic. Some people may not like to write blog posts, but including your Periscopes, YouTube videos, podcasts, or other content pieces in a blog format is also a good way to keep fresh eyes coming to your site. After each post, you can be collecting emails and promoting your opt-ins. 'End-Content' is a Wordpress plugin available and Popup Ally also has this option. If you have Squarespace, you can manually add sign up forms at the end of each article.

Action Item: Create a signup form for your opt-in to ensure you are capturing information after every single blog post.

CONTENT UPGRADES

Remember when I said that your opt-in needed to be general? Your content upgrades are where you get super specific. On my site, I create content for side hustlers who may treat their business as an extra stream of income and those who may want to transition into full-time entrepreneurship. Both audiences are not the same and require some content created specifically for them. For example, I have job search articles and resources like the Paper Chase course that may not be appealing to those who want to go into business full-time. By using a freebie that is so specific to a particular audience as an opt-in product, I limit the amount of people that will subscribe. This is where content upgrades come in.

Content upgrades are incentives related to a specific topic that are available for download. For example, I have content upgrades for various topics on my site. Like job search email templates and a video on building your LinkedIn profile. These content upgrades are available within blog posts in the job search category. My freebies like the Instagram Photography Guide for Business Owners is available in blog posts about business and social media. Makes sense? Opt-ins apply to your entire audience and are used site-wide to drive subscriptions, while content upgrades are used within specific blog posts and apply to a specific subset of your audience.

Here are 12 ideas for content upgrades you can add to your existing blog posts and guest posts to get more email subscribers:

• Private resources page.
• Templates and worksheets.
• Video of you talking about a few extra points and details.
• Calendar or excel spreadsheet.
• Desktop background.
• Relevant or adjacent guide.
• Done-for-you scripts for email or phone.
• Code or swipe files you use.
• Excerpt chapter from your eBook.
• Audio or video interview with the subject of your blog post.

Once you know what your content upgrades will be, you need to figure out how you're going to implement them into your site. There are multiple options.
You can use a form from a tool like SumoMe or your email provider. For Squarespace, you can use the Squarespace Newsletter Block. And if you are balling, you can use LeadBoxes from LeadPages.

Action Item: Create a content upgrade for the top three blog posts on your site. Since these posts already get the most traffic, you should capitalize on it by capturing emails.

SEARCH

When you create a website, you need to write for two different audiences: for people and for search engines. What does this mean? It means that your content and pages need to balance your personality and value with keywords for search engine optimization. You should always write with a keyword in mind and this keyword should appear in a few key places:

• Title of post or page.
• URL of post or page.
• Meta description.
• Heading within page (that's what H1, H2, and so on are for in the formatting section)
• The first paragraph of your content.
• The last paragraph of your content.
• As a hyperlink within you page.
• Images (Name of the image, image description, alt text).

What is SEO? Search engine optimization is the process of improving the visibility of your website on search engine results. Not many of us click past the first few pages of search results and SEO is a way to ensure your site appears closer and closer to the top of the results. For all you digital foreigners, you are probably already thinking that SEO is too difficult for you to understand. Here are some tips.

1. Don't overwhelm your pages with graphics.
Take a good hard look at your website. Anything text that is in a graphic or flash animation will not be read by the search engines. Is your logo the only place your name appears? Then you are virtually invisible. For the graphics that you do have, be sure to include alternative 'alt' text describing what the photo is and have image names for each.

2. Create content.
Blogging is an important part of optimizing your site. By adding new content, you increase the amount of relevant information on your site. Search engines like constantly updated pages with longer text because it is usually more beneficial to the reader. Make sure you include your name with each post.

3. Share your content everywhere.
Share on social media more than once. A tweet doesn't last more than a few hours online. Constantly share your content on Twitter, Facebook and LinkedIn to ensure you are reaching the most people. Bookmarking sites like Digg and Delicious also help increase traffic to your site. Include your blog in your email signature and anywhere else that people can click through to read it.

Now, if you're a Wordpress user, you're in luck. You can install the Yoast SEO plugin, which will help you optimize all your posts. It will rank your post and pages red, yellow, or green and make suggestions on how to improve for your specific keyword or phrase. If you don't have Wordpress, you will have to manually ensure that you have your keyword in as many of the places mentioned above as possible. Here is a one pager you can print and keep as a reminder.

Action Item: Identify the keywords that are important to your business and brand. Be as specific as possible. What would people type into Google to find your products, services or site?

SOCIAL
Social media is important for multiple reasons. Not only are those channels part of search engines themselves, they are also a place where new people can discover your content. The tool that I recently started using that helped me double my traffic and followers is called CoSchedule and is worth every penny (there's also a free trial available so definitely take advantage of that). It allows you to streamline the sharing of your content. Most people share their blog posts a few times and then forget about it. With CoSchedule, you can schedule posts very easily for long periods of time.

I like to schedule posts to be shared on Twitter and LinkedIn on publish, the day after, 3 days after, a week later, 2 weeks later, 28 days later and a month after publishing. For other channels like Instagram, I might share it once and again a month after. Sometimes, if the post is doing very well, I will schedule it out more times. The key to keeping content fresh and sharing it this many times is to nail down copy creation. I take the same blog post title and write it out 5-9 different ways. The variation in copy and presentation will capture readers' attention. You can use them on variations channels as well.

1. Ask a question.
2. End the update with a question.
3. Include a fill-in-the-blank question.
4. Write it in a sentence.
5. Use relevant hashtags in the update.
6. Attribute and tag other accounts.
7. Include a comment.
8. Pull a statistic or quote from article.
9. Switch the title around.

Here is what that would look like in practice:

Original post and link: The 2 Enlightening Twitter Metrics We Often Ignore
http://bit.ly/1L001wX

1. **Ask a question:** Not sure what to do with all those #Twitter metrics? Here are two insights to watch: http://bit.ly/1L001wX
2. **End the update with a question:** The 2 Enlightening Twitter Metrics We Often Ignore http://bit.ly/1L001wX – have you ever considered these important?
3. **Include a fill-in-the-blank question:** _____ + _____ are two important #Twittermetrics to monitor (Find out which metrics matter most here http://bit.ly/1L001wX)

4. **Write it in a sentence:** The are 2 enlightening Twitter metrics that you shouldn't ignore **http://bit.ly/1L001wX**
5. **Use relevant hashtags in the update:** The 2 Enlightening Twitter Metrics We Often Ignore http://bit.ly/1L001wX #socialmediaanalytics #data #cmgr
6. **Attribute and tag other accounts:** The 2 Metrics You Are Ignoring http://bit.ly/aVd9s6 by @emmeliedelacruz
7. **Include a comment:** Never thought about this. Easy way to find your most influential and interactive users: **http://bit.ly/1L001wX**
8. **Pull a statistic or quote from article:** According to Nielsen, 92% of consumers trust recommendations over advertising. These metrics show how well you're doing in this area: **http://bit.ly/1L001wX**
9. **Switch the title around**: Metrics You Can't Ignore on Twitter http://bit.ly/1L001wX

Action Item: Take your best performing blog post and rewrite the title at least 5 different ways and schedule across social media throughout the rest of the month.

SHARE

The second most important aspect of SEO is quality inbound links. Inbound links are links on other sites that point back to your site, and they are one of the most significant aspects of getting your website ranked higher in search engines. Obtaining quality inbound links is probably one of the harder aspects of blogging; the best inbound links come from sites that are difficult to get featured on. The most obvious way to get these inbound links is by looking for guest posting opportunities and features on high quality sites. Social media also helps with this. Ultimately, it's all about driving traffic to your site.

Guest posting is all about relationship building, and we will get to that in another challenge or webinar. What you need to know is that you should be pitching your content to other blogs and sites to get in front of new eyes and get the search engine benefit. That's not so simple and takes time. Below are 2 quick things you can do today to get your shares up.

When other people share your content, it is a form of social proof. To get people to share your posts, you have to make it easy for them to do so with a tool like Click to Tweet. It is both a website that anyone can use and a Wordpress plugin. I use it on my site, landing pages and emails to encourage sharing. When people click the link, a tweet is auto-generated for them, so all they have to do is hit send.

Another thing that your website must do to encourage sharing is have a Pin-it button or some form of social sharing button.

Action Item: Make your content shareable and ensure you have sharing buttons readily available throughout your site. Update your latest blog posts with some snippets to share. (Psst, it can be the same copy that you created yesterday).

ABOUT PAGE

Your *About Page* needs to first and foremost exist. I just did a website audit the other day where the website didn't have two of the things that we are going to discuss in this email. Your 'About' page is the first page you should create on your website because it is what is going to stop you from being anonymous. Why are people going to pay you if they have no clue who you are or how you are qualified to help them?

This page doesn't need to be overwhelming or intimidating either. All you need is a clear, crisp headshot, a short paragraph about you, your best content, your contact information, and a call to action. Do you want them to sign up for your newsletter, follow you on social media, and visit your YouTube account? Tell people what to do next. Keywords are also important here. How are people going to find you? Be sure to include the right sets of words and phrases that your target audience might be googling with.

To write a kick-ass bio, create an inventory of your skills and accomplishments. What problem do you love to solve at work or for others? How are you the aspirin to someone's pain? What proof do you have that what you say is true? How have you done this successfully before and what are the facts and statistics to back it up? What skills do you have to do this? What do you want to do next with this valuable skill? Where do you see potential for this skill to be of great value (i.e. save or make significant money, time, energy) for your audience?

Use the template to begin writing a bio that will make a great 1st impression. Notice I said, begin. This template is best used on your LinkedIn profile and media kit. It is very professional in nature. After you have all your facts together, you will want to make it personal and impactful to your audience. You want them to feel like you understand them and like you're on the same page.

_____ is a _____ (what you do) who helps _____ (problem you solve and who you solve it for). As a _____ (your expertise or notable achievement), _____(proof of your expertise and ability to solve stated problem using skills or past accomplishments). _____(name) currently _____ (what you currently do) and _____ (value you have added to your organization or team). For more information/to contact _____ (Contact information).

Example:
Elizabeth Grant is a digital marketing professional that creates audience driven campaigns for non- profit organizations. As a professional working in the marketing industry for 5 years, she has worked with clients such as the Make a Wish Foundation and the Boys and Girls Club of America increasing their engagement on channels, such as Twitter and Facebook. Elizabeth currently works for an agency where she has learned to manage online communities and is skilled in proving her return on investment through

the reporting and metric processes she has developed. For more information, visit her website elizabethgrant.com

Here's my professional bio.
Emmelie De La Cruz is a personal branding expert and author of 'Make Yourself Marketable'. After working in various areas of marketing and communication, she launched her consultancy, The Branding Muse that specializes in personal branding and social media. Her insights have been featured in Cosmo for Latinas, Black Enterprise, Lisa Evers' Street Soldiers, The Miami Herald, The Huffington Post, PR Daily, and Forbes named her site one of the top career websites in 2013. Emmelie's clients have included executives, politicians, speakers and media personalities as well as college students and young professionals. She has spoken at various universities, events and organizations and trained thousands of millennials on building their personal brand and digital identities through various social media tools. Meet Emmelie on Twitter (@EmmelieDeLaCruz) or learn more at emmeliedelacruz.com.

Now head over to my site and take a look at the bio I have there. Similar, but more personal.

Action Item: Create or recreate your About Page with a bomb bio.

CONTACT PAGE
Another often forgotten page is the contact page. Don't forget to include your contact info and links to your social media. Even if you have a contact form, you should still always put your email address and other ways to keep in touch. Make it easy for them to reach out to you. If it's easy for people to find you, it's easier for opportunities to find you. More importantly, use this to showcase a little more social proof. List the brands you've worked with, testimonials for your clients, or even screenshots of feedback that you've gotten. Remind people why they wanted to contact you in the first place.

Action Item: Take a look at your contact page. In addition to just having a contact form, describe the best way to contact you and provide all the necessary information. Take the guesswork out of finding you.

OFFERING PAGE
Services and Shop pages are an introduction to your offerings. It should not be overwhelming to the eye or very distracting. Focus on outlining the benefits of working with you and exactly what is included in the product or service. Simplify the shopper's experience so they can easily find what they are looking for. Highlight things like price, clearly list the features and benefits, and have payment buttons installed on your site. If people have to take extra steps to purchase from you, you might lose a customer. Again, make it easy for people. You can use a Shortcodes plugin to easily create buttons that match the aesthetic of your site. Do not, and I repeat, do not have the rachet looking

PayPal button on your site. It's tacky. Create custom buttons using a plugin like Zilla Shortcodes or WooCommerce. Squarespace has a built-in button tool as well.

Action Item: Restructure your Shop or Services page to include photos and purchase buttons for each item or service. Make it easy for the page to be quickly scanned and call out key information.

LINKS

I am going to continue hammering home the message of making it easy for people to buy from you. It really is what makes all the difference. You do amazing work (I hope), but if people can't get to it, you can't make money. This is where your products and services links come in. This book is available at emmeliedelacruz.com/planner. I can easily tell someone the link, and they can find it on their own. If I expected someone to go to my site, type in Profit Planner, find my book, and then buy it, I may be making way less money. The fewer steps to purchase, the better. Simplify the links on your site and create shortlinks for overly complicated URLs.

Use a Wordpress plugin like Pretty Links or a tool like Bit.ly to shorten and customize your links so they are easy to remember. Use one or two words after your domain with Pretty Links (example: www.YourWebsite.com/Word) to make them easy to remember, or customize the Bit.ly link to be easy to type. Shortlinks are very helpful in sharing and remembering.

Action Item: Create links for your top 3 offerings.

TRACKING

Now, in addition to selling your own products and services, you can also sell other people's product and services through affiliate links. What is an affiliate link? It is a link that allows you to get paid for a referral. You can have affiliate links for all kinds of things from tools to clothes to books. You can monetize your whole entire life with affiliate links. What does this have to do with your website? You could be leaving money on the table if you aren't taking advantage of links. Track your best performing content and sprinkle some affiliate links in there. For example, my #1 post for the last few years has been 'How to Contact Recruiters During the Job Search'. In that post, I include an affiliate link to guide people to resume templates. Why? Because it is an organic recommendation. Can you create a product or service around what people already engage with? Are there affiliate links you can include in your already written posts? Read up on affiliate marketing here.

If you want an automated inclusion of links, which I recommend, use a plugin like Auto Affiliate Links or a service like SkimLinks. Every single day, I miss this plugin a ton. It is golden. I have to manually add all my links to Squarespace. When I hack that platform, I will let y'all know!

Action Item: Track your best performing content and pages and see if there is a trend. Include 1 or 2 affiliate links in that content.

PAYMENT PROCESSORS

Sales tools can get overwhelming and complicated if you don't know what you are looking for. To be able to take payments, you need a payment processor. That means: PayPal, Square, Stripe or Braintree. These are the main ones used online, but there are also platforms like Selz and Gumroad that work well for you if you are delivering digital products. In addition to these tools, you can also use shopping carts like WooCommerce or DPD (Digital Product Delivery) to sell multiple items. Both work with PayPal.

Because this is the Profit Planner, and I know you are here for the shortcuts and the answers, I'm going to give it to you straight. From my research and a ton of trial and error, I have found that PayPal, Selz and WooCommerce work the best and are the easiest to deal with when you have Wordpress. When I had Wordpress, I would use PayPal in combination with WooCommerce to sell physical and digital products. Selz, I used as an alternative for people who didn't have PayPal. In addition to these, I also use the Wave accounting site to create and send invoices when I am providing a service.

Squarespace has Stripe and PayPal payments built-in, so you don't have to worry about it.

Audit of all the products and services you want to sell. How easy or difficult is the checkout process? Are you sending your customers to a few different pages? Is the process easy to follow or understand? We must make it easy for people to find and purchase our products whether digital or physical. Nicole Walters, also known as Scoprah on Periscope, has one page with all her digital products on, which makes it easy for people to find when she refers to them on her Periscopes.

Action Item: Set up a shop page and make it easy for people to purchase what you sell with buy buttons and a smooth checkout process.

SALES TOOLS

In addition to selling on your website, you should increase your exposure through 3rd party marketplaces. The more places you sell, the better. Yesterday you focused on the tools to sell on your website. Today, we are going to talk about external sales tools. Why do you need them? They already have a built-in customer base that you can tap into and monetize. Instead of simply selling to the audience that is on your site, you can use the sites below to list your products and services, while they do the marketing for you. There is strength in numbers and using sites like this can increase your sales and exposure to new clients.

- If you are a creative and design templates or other graphics: Creative Market.
- If you teach courses: UDemy, Coursera, Skillshare, Teachable, Thinkific.
- Makeup or Beauty Services: StyleSeat.

- Books: Amazon via Createspace.
- Merchandise: Printful (sell merchandise without holding inventory), Etsy, Zazzle, TeeSpring.
- Freelancing or Services: Fiverr, UpWork, Cloudpeeps.
- Coaching: Clarity.FM, Sevpal.

Action Item: List your products or services on at least one third-party marketplace.

MEASUREMENT

I get it! You might not consider yourself a data nerd like I do. While I hate math, analyzing numbers makes me super excited. Wordpress does a great job providing built-in analytics for you through the Jetpack Plugin on your dashboard, but you shouldn't just be looking at the pretty graphs and numbers. You want to monitor key areas to make better decisions about your site. Take a look at the screenshots from my site below. These are the stats for my best performing day last week. If you're getting less than 1K views per day, you can look at your stats for the best-performing week.

You want to take a look at your referrals. (I had a spike in traffic and wasn't sure why. Had I not looked at this, I wouldn't have known that I was featured in a Brit and Co article that day. This is important because you want to know where you audience is coming from.)

You also want to look at your Top Posts and Pages, Clicks and Search Terms. These will inform what your audience is doing on your site and indicates what's working and what's interesting. If you started using affiliate links, you will see what people are clicking on most and can include that link in more content.

Action Item: Make note of your best performing post or page over the last week and your top search engine term was and use that information to create another post on the same topic using the search term. Take a look at what your best performing link is. Where is it located on your site and how can you replicate this success?

GOOGLE ANALYTICS

You should have already installed Google Analytics onto your site; if you haven't, then you need to get it done ASAP. Once you have it, you're going to set up goals in your account. So, what are goals? Goals are things that you want to happen on your website and a way of measuring the completion of those actions. For example, my goals are having people sign up for my newsletter and purchase my book. I want to know how many out of the 10K people that visit my site each month, end up joining my email list or buying something.

In order to do this, you will need to map out your goals and the destination after that action is completed. When you sign up for my newsletter, you are taken to a 'Thank you' page. When you purchase my book, you are redirected to an 'Order Received' page. Where are you taking your buyers? If you do not have a page that you redirect them to, create one. These are called destination pages. You will need it to set your goals in Google Analytics. Here is the thank you page when people sign up for my list.

You can have one destination page that you drive people to regardless of what they purchased, or create an individual one for each item you sell. It all depends how you want to measure. You should also create a destination page for when people sign up for your newsletter. You might include the link to this page as part of your form settings in Mailchimp or whatever email service provider you use.

Action Item: Create the destination pages for your goals and watch my YouTube tutorial to get those set up in Google Analytics. It's a lot easier than you think, promise.

WELCOME BAR
There are many ways to increase your conversion. Here's another one. Add a welcome bar at the top of your website, and include calls to actions, such as sharing your post, subscribing to your newsletter, or checking out a new product or service. That way, people can have easy access to the pages and links that are most important for you.

Action Item: Install the AddThis Welcome Bar plugin on Wordpress or the built in Announcement Bar on Squarespace and customize it to promote either your shop page or your funnel freebie.

SIDEBAR AND FOOTER
The sidebar and footer are one of the most underutilized areas of your website. These two areas are golden because they do something that only the navigation bar does: exist on every page. People need to see things repeatedly, so your most important Calls to Action should exist in this area. From your opt-in forms, to your best-selling products, to your upcoming class, the sidebar needs to literally haunt people throughout your entire site to get them closer to converting. The top widgets that you should include in your sidebar are:

- An Image and HTML Box promoting your opt-in product and capturing information.
- Your Most Popular Posts.
- Your social media channel.
- Any ads to affiliate content or your products and services.

Action Item: Get your sidebar and footer together. Maximize this space to create value for your website.

MAXIMIZING BLOG POSTS

If you are just writing and publishing blog posts and that's it, you are doing it all wrong! You need to repurpose content in new ways to keep your readers engaged. You can maximize your blog posts by including a slideshow, video, podcast or pdf. Similar to content upgrades, these kinds of content are education pieces that further add to your credibility and make people more likely to convert. They open people's eyes to the need for your product or service or showcase your product in action. They include: case studies, reports, tutorials, testimonials, swipe copy etc. By adding one of these elements to your high-performing blog posts, you will be able to make people more likely to convert and take whatever action you want them to.

Action Item: Add an education element to your top three blog posts. It should further prove why your product or service is a good fit, or works for the brand.

CALLS TO ACTION

Your website fails to convert, because you don't make it obvious what you want and need people to do. But don't feel bad, most people don't.

- 70% of small business websites don't display clear calls to action for anything on their home pages, such as such as specials, e-mail newsletters, how-to guides etc.
- 72% don't have any calls to action on their interior pages like the About page, contact page or even the blog.

Without telling people the action you want them to take, how do you expect them to take any at all? As I've mentioned before, humans are lazy. They want things with as little effort as possible. Include 'calls to action', easy to identify links, a clear and simple navigation menu, and anything else you can think of that will encourage people to browse through your site. If you make something hard for a reader to find, that person will get frustrated and look for the answers to their problems elsewhere.

Get bossy and tell people what to do. Speak CTAs fluently. What does that mean? Call to actions: learn them; love them; use them. And because, I'm all about the HOW, not the WHAT, here are some guidelines to help you write the best call to actions. We went over these in the social media section, but here is a refresher using website examples.

Lead with a clear action:
"Click below to share this blog post" vs. "Share this blog post."

Focus on one thing:
"Call us to sign up for a free consultation." vs. "Fill out this form and email us to schedule a time to chat."

Create a sense of urgency:
"Purchase this product in the next 7 days to take advantage of early bird pricing. Prices will double after the deadline."

Give them a reason why or an outcome:
"Join the challenge" vs. "Join the challenge and grow your following in 30 days"
'Buy Now' vs. "Click Here to Save 5 Hours a Week."
"Download Now" or "Get Your Free White Paper Instantly"

Use suspense:
"I share even more detail in my emails and on my InstaStories. Join me! (@EmmelieDeLaCruz)" vs. "Sign up for my newsletter and follow me on Instagram."
"Sign up to get this free resource" vs. "Show Me the Content".

Provide instant gratification:
"Sign up for the class" vs. "Sign up and get the 1st class immediately in your inbox."

Marie Forleo's website is the best site when it comes to calls to actions. She has a simple website that gets the job done and focuses on one primary thing: getting people on her email list. What are you focusing on?

Action Item: Reformat your navigation bar to include the top 5 areas of your site you want people to focus on and include one call to action on your About page and homepage. Remember, your footer and sidebar are a great place for this.

RETARGETING
Have you ever been on a website, left the website, and then saw a Facebook or Instagram advertisement of the exact same thing you were just looking at?
That's retargeting. Retargeting is Internet stalking basically.

It works by using a tracking code called a 'pixel' to keep track of the people who visit your site. If that person visits a certain page and doesn't buy, they will be followed around the internet by your ads on places like Facebook, Instagram, or other blogs. This is a great strategy to support your email funnels.

Action Item: Explore retargeting on a tool called AdRoll, or hire a freelancer on Fiverr to get you all set up. Spend a small amount to test this method of closing sales.

NOW, LET'S GET TO THIS MONEY...

PRODUCT CREATION

PROBLEM

What is a problem that my audience is struggling with now?

AUDIENCE

Who has this problem?

PRODUCT

What will I create, repackage, or revamp to solve the problem.

PRODUCT TYPE
Book/eBook
Email Challenge
Online Course
Webinar
Product
Program
Other:

OUTLINE + CONTENT IDEAS

What is going in it? Think of this as the table of contents for your product.

SALES PAGE OUTLINE

HEADLINE

PROBLEM

PAIN POINT

OFFER

PRICING

TESTIMONIALS

ABOUT ME

QUALIFICATION

FREEBIE

FAQS

THE MONEY MAP

VALIDATION

Before I spend time and resources creating the thing I just outlined on the previous page, I will contact at least...

_____ *in the hope that* _____ *purchase by* _____
TARGETS   PRE-SALE CUSTOMERS   DEADLINE

Example: I will contact at least 100 people in the hope that 15 purchase by next Friday.

CONVERSIONS

Based on what happened during your pre-sale period, you can set goals for the real deal.

_____ *divided by* _____ *means I have a* _____
BUYERS   VISITORS   CONVERSION RATE

Example: 17 customers, out of the 75 people that saw the landing page means my conversion rate is: 22.6%

REVENUE

Now let's talk money.
How much do you want?

_____ *divided by* _____ *means I must sell* _____
MONTHLY GOALS   PRICE OF PRODUCT   SALES GOALS

Example: To make $5000 from a $39 product, I must sell 128 of them in a month.

TRAFFIC

With your revenue goal and your conversion rate, you can how much work is needed.

_____ *divided by* _____ *means I need* _____
SALES GOAL   CONVERSION RATE   LANDING PAGE VISITS

Example: To get 128 customers with a 22.6% conversion rate, I need to send 566 people to my landing page.

SOCIAL MEDIA PLAN

THINGS TO PROMOTE

TOPICS	SOCIAL POSTS	

NURTURE PLAN

FREEBIE

How can I begin to solve the problem for my audience without giving it all away?

TYPE
eBook
Challenge
Mini-Course
Webinar
Discount
Quiz
Other:

TRIPWIRE

What can I sell for under $30 that will further help my audience solve their problem?

BONUSES

What can I offer that will create a sense of urgency for my audience to buy within a specific timeframe?

DOWNSELL

What will be my last attempt to close the sale? What else can I offer to help solve their problem?

CONTENT IDEAS

EMAIL 1

Describe the problem then showcase the solution.

To Dos and Logistics

EMAIL 2

Share a way to solve the problem and present your product as a possble solution.

To Dos and Logistics

EMAIL 3

Invite them to purchase your offer and share the benefits.

To Dos and Logistics

EMAIL 4

Share a client/customer success story or your own personal success story.

To Dos and Logistics

EMAIL 5

Combat any rebuttals and answer any frequently asked questions.

To Dos and Logistics

EMAIL 6

Cart Closing Email

To Dos and Logistics

EMAIL 7

Last Chance Email

To Dos and Logistics

EMAIL 8

Downsell Email

To Dos and Logistics

THE MONTH'S MASTER PLAN

SUNDAY	MONDAY	TUESDAY	WEDNESDAY	THURSDAY	FRIDAY	SATURDAY

FREEBIE OUTLINE

TITLE

PRODUCT TYPE
eBook
Email Challenge
Webinar
Coupon/Discount
Other:

INTRO

PROBLEM

SOLUTION

OFFER

FREEBIE PAGE OUTLINE

HEADLINE

TEASER BULLETS AND DETAILS

FORM

CTA

TRIPWIRE OUTLINE

TITLE

PRODUCT TYPE

eBook	Whitepaper
Email Challenge	Report
Online Course	Coupon/Discount
Webinar	Other:

INTRO

PROBLEM

SOLUTION

OFFER

TRIPWIRE PAGE OUTLINE

THANK YOU

OFFER + DETAILS

SOCIAL PROOF

CTA

MASTER CHECKLIST

WEEK 1: THINGS TO WRITE
○ Social media schedule to drive traffic to free blog posts, lead magnet and offering sales page at least 20 days worth of promoting.
○ Free blog posts and/or podcast episodes
○ Lead magnet or freebie (ebook, email challenge, quiz, webinar, tutorial, checklist)
○ Lead magnet delivery email
○ Nurture sequence email funnel
○ Offering delivery sequence email
○ Sales page video
○ Create promo codes, countdowns, and landing pages for any bonuses

○ WEEK 2:THINGS TO DESIGN
○ Banner images for your landing pages
○ Cover graphic for your video
○ Mockups of your product, deliverables, or freebie
○ Flyer sharing your freebie
○ Blog post promotion graphics
○ Flyer for social media announcing the offering
○ Graphic with a testimonial on it
○ Flyer announcing the offering with the early bird price
○ Mockups of your product or deliverables from your service
○ Flash sale graphic
○ Instagram story/Snapchat/Pinterest versions of all of the above

WEEK 3: THINGS TO MAKE
○ Sales page
○ Lead magnet landing page
○ Lead magnet email sequence (delivery)
○ 3-5 email nurture funnel
○ Core offer sales page
○ Core offer email sequence (delivery + nurture funnel)
○ Webinar replay page
○ Create UTM tags for all links
○ Setup special promotions such as early bird prices or fast-action bonuses
○ Test all links, automations and email deliveries

WEEK 4: LAUNCH FLOW
○ Send an email to your current email list announcing the product or service.
○ Release a new blog post/video/podcast at least once a week during the promotion period.
○ Promote blog posts and freebie to capture emails and interest daily.
○ Potential customer downloads freebie and is added to an email list.
○ Potential customer receives email with freebie and email briefly mentions offering.
○ Potential customer is sent 3-7 emails promoting the product or service.
○ Customer that buys is removed from email list and added to an email list for the service.
○ Potential customer that hasn't purchase receives a flash sale or last chance email.
○ Update your funnel to make them evergreen, if needed.

AMPLIFICATION

INFLUENCERS	PARTNERS	PROMOTION/CAMPAIGN

AFFILIATES	SPONSORED/GUEST CONTENT

OTHER IDEAS

YOU GOT THIS!

REVENUE GOAL

PRIORITIES	INFLUENCE AND INCOME	**MINDSET MANTRA**
○		
○		
○		

MORNING

AFTERNOON

EVENING

CALLS / EMAILS / TEXTS

LET'S REVIEW

○ FEEL ACCOMPLISHED?   ○ NOURISHED YOURSELF?   ○ PREPARE FOR TOMORROW?

WITH LOVE, *Emmelie*

YOU GOT THIS!

REVENUE GOAL

PRIORITIES	INFLUENCE AND INCOME	**MINDSET MANTRA**
○		
○		
○		

MORNING

AFTERNOON

EVENING

CALLS / EMAILS / TEXTS

LET'S REVIEW

 ◯ FEEL ACCOMPLISHED?   ◯ NOURISHED YOURSELF?   ◯ PREPARE FOR TOMORROW?

 WITH LOVE, *Emmelie*

NOTES AND REFLECTIONS

YOU GOT THIS!

REVENUE GOAL

PRIORITIES	INFLUENCE AND INCOME	**MINDSET MANTRA**
○		
○		
○		

MORNING

AFTERNOON

EVENING

CALLS / EMAILS / TEXTS

LET'S REVIEW

○ FEEL ACCOMPLISHED? ○ NOURISHED YOURSELF? ○ PREPARE FOR TOMORROW?

WITH LOVE, Emmelie

NOTES AND REFLECTIONS

YOU GOT THIS!

REVENUE GOAL

PRIORITIES	INFLUENCE AND INCOME	**MINDSET MANTRA**
○		
○		
○		

MORNING

AFTERNOON

EVENING

CALLS / EMAILS / TEXTS

LET'S REVIEW

○ FEEL ACCOMPLISHED?   ○ NOURISHED YOURSELF?   ○ PREPARE FOR TOMORROW?

WITH LOVE, *Emmelie*

NOTES AND REFLECTIONS

YOU GOT THIS!

REVENUE GOAL

PRIORITIES	INFLUENCE AND INCOME	**MINDSET MANTRA**
○		
○		
○		

MORNING

AFTERNOON

EVENING

CALLS / EMAILS / TEXTS

LET'S REVIEW

○ FEEL ACCOMPLISHED?　　　○ NOURISHED YOURSELF?　　　○ PREPARE FOR TOMORROW?

WITH LOVE, *Emmelie*

NOTES AND REFLECTIONS

YOU GOT THIS!

REVENUE GOAL

PRIORITIES	INFLUENCE AND INCOME	**MINDSET MANTRA**
O		
O		
O		

MORNING

AFTERNOON

EVENING

CALLS / EMAILS / TEXTS

LET'S REVIEW

 FEEL ACCOMPLISHED?   *NOURISHED YOURSELF?*   ◯ *PREPARE FOR TOMORROW?*

WITH LOVE, Emmelie

YOU GOT THIS!

REVENUE GOAL

PRIORITIES	INFLUENCE AND INCOME	**MINDSET MANTRA**
○		
○		
○		

MORNING

AFTERNOON

EVENING

CALLS / EMAILS / TEXTS

LET'S REVIEW

○ FEEL ACCOMPLISHED?   ○ NOURISHED YOURSELF?   ○ PREPARE FOR TOMORROW?

WITH LOVE, *Emmelie*

YOU GOT THIS!

REVENUE GOAL

PRIORITIES	INFLUENCE AND INCOME	**MINDSET MANTRA**
○		
○		
○		

MORNING

AFTERNOON

EVENING

CALLS / EMAILS / TEXTS

LET'S REVIEW

○ FEEL ACCOMPLISHED?   ○ NOURISHED YOURSELF?   ○ PREPARE FOR TOMORROW?

WITH LOVE, *Emmelie*

NOTES AND REFLECTIONS

YOU GOT THIS!

REVENUE GOAL

PRIORITIES	INFLUENCE AND INCOME	**MINDSET MANTRA**
○		
○		
○		

MORNING

AFTERNOON

EVENING

CALLS / EMAILS / TEXTS

LET'S REVIEW

○ FEEL ACCOMPLISHED?   ○ NOURISHED YOURSELF?   ○ PREPARE FOR TOMORROW?

WITH LOVE, *Emmelie*

NOTES AND REFLECTIONS

YOU GOT THIS!

REVENUE GOAL

PRIORITIES	INFLUENCE AND INCOME	**MINDSET MANTRA**
○		
○		
○		

MORNING

AFTERNOON

EVENING

CALLS / EMAILS / TEXTS

LET'S REVIEW

○ FEEL ACCOMPLISHED?　　○ NOURISHED YOURSELF?　　○ PREPARE FOR TOMORROW?

WITH LOVE, *Emmelie*

YOU GOT THIS!

REVENUE GOAL

PRIORITIES	INFLUENCE AND INCOME	**MINDSET MANTRA**
○		
○		
○		

MORNING

AFTERNOON

EVENING

CALLS / EMAILS / TEXTS

LET'S REVIEW

○ FEEL ACCOMPLISHED?   ○ NOURISHED YOURSELF?   ○ PREPARE FOR TOMORROW?

WITH LOVE, *Emmelie*

NOTES AND REFLECTIONS

YOU GOT THIS!

REVENUE GOAL

PRIORITIES	INFLUENCE AND INCOME	**MINDSET MANTRA**
○		
○		
○		

MORNING

AFTERNOON

EVENING

CALLS / EMAILS / TEXTS

LET'S REVIEW

○ FEEL ACCOMPLISHED?   ○ NOURISHED YOURSELF?   ○ PREPARE FOR TOMORROW?

WITH LOVE, Emmelie

NOTES AND
REFLECTIONS

YOU GOT THIS!

REVENUE GOAL

PRIORITIES	INFLUENCE AND INCOME	**MINDSET MANTRA**
○		
○		
○		

MORNING

AFTERNOON

EVENING

CALLS / EMAILS / TEXTS

LET'S REVIEW

○ FEEL ACCOMPLISHED?   ○ NOURISHED YOURSELF?   ○ PREPARE FOR TOMORROW?

WITH LOVE, *Emmelie*

YOU GOT THIS!

REVENUE GOAL

PRIORITIES	INFLUENCE AND INCOME	**MINDSET MANTRA**
○		
○		
○		

MORNING

AFTERNOON

EVENING

CALLS / EMAILS / TEXTS

LET'S REVIEW

◯ FEEL ACCOMPLISHED?   ◯ NOURISHED YOURSELF?   ◯ PREPARE FOR TOMORROW?

WITH LOVE, *Emmelie*

NOTES AND REFLECTIONS

YOU GOT THIS!

REVENUE GOAL

PRIORITIES	INFLUENCE AND INCOME	**MINDSET MANTRA**
○		
○		
○		

MORNING

AFTERNOON

EVENING

CALLS / EMAILS / TEXTS

LET'S REVIEW

○ FEEL ACCOMPLISHED?   ○ NOURISHED YOURSELF?   ○ PREPARE FOR TOMORROW?

WITH LOVE, *Emmelie*

YOU GOT THIS!

PRIORITIES	INFLUENCE AND INCOME	**MINDSET MANTRA**
○		
○		
○		

MORNING

AFTERNOON

EVENING

CALLS / EMAILS / TEXTS

LET'S REVIEW

○ FEEL ACCOMPLISHED?   ○ NOURISHED YOURSELF?   ○ PREPARE FOR TOMORROW?

WITH LOVE, *Emmelie*

YOU GOT THIS!

REVENUE GOAL

PRIORITIES	INFLUENCE AND INCOME	**MINDSET MANTRA**
○		
○		
○		

MORNING

AFTERNOON

EVENING

CALLS / EMAILS / TEXTS

LET'S REVIEW

○ FEEL ACCOMPLISHED?　　○ NOURISHED YOURSELF?　　○ PREPARE FOR TOMORROW?

WITH LOVE, *Emmelie*

NOTES AND REFLECTIONS

YOU GOT THIS!

REVENUE GOAL

PRIORITIES	INFLUENCE AND INCOME	**MINDSET MANTRA**
○		
○		
○		

MORNING

AFTERNOON

EVENING

CALLS / EMAILS / TEXTS

LET'S REVIEW

◯ FEEL ACCOMPLISHED?   ◯ NOURISHED YOURSELF?   ◯ PREPARE FOR TOMORROW?

WITH LOVE, *Emmelie*

NOTES AND REFLECTIONS

YOU GOT THIS!

REVENUE GOAL

PRIORITIES	INFLUENCE AND INCOME	**MINDSET MANTRA**
O		
O		
O		

MORNING

AFTERNOON

EVENING

CALLS / EMAILS / TEXTS

LET'S REVIEW

 FEEL ACCOMPLISHED?   NOURISHED YOURSELF? ◯ PREPARE FOR TOMORROW?

WITH LOVE, *Emmelie*

YOU GOT THIS!

REVENUE GOAL

PRIORITIES	INFLUENCE AND INCOME	**MINDSET MANTRA**
○		
○		
○		

MORNING

AFTERNOON

EVENING

CALLS / EMAILS / TEXTS

LET'S REVIEW

○ FEEL ACCOMPLISHED?   ○ NOURISHED YOURSELF?   ○ PREPARE FOR TOMORROW?

WITH LOVE, *Emmelie*

NOTES AND REFLECTIONS

YOU GOT THIS!

REVENUE GOAL

PRIORITIES	INFLUENCE AND INCOME	**MINDSET MANTRA**
○		
○		
○		

MORNING

AFTERNOON

EVENING

CALLS / EMAILS / TEXTS

LET'S REVIEW

○ FEEL ACCOMPLISHED?   ○ NOURISHED YOURSELF?   ○ PREPARE FOR TOMORROW?

WITH LOVE, *Emmelie*

NOTES AND REFLECTIONS

YOU GOT THIS!

PRIORITIES	INFLUENCE AND INCOME	MINDSET MANTRA
O		
O		
O		

MORNING	CALLS / EMAILS / TEXTS

AFTERNOON

EVENING

LET'S REVIEW

O FEEL ACCOMPLISHED?　　　O NOURISHED YOURSELF?　　　O PREPARE FOR TOMORROW?

WITH LOVE, *Emmelie*

NOTES AND REFLECTIONS

YOU GOT THIS!

REVENUE GOAL

PRIORITIES	INFLUENCE AND INCOME	**MINDSET MANTRA**
○		
○		
○		

MORNING

AFTERNOON

EVENING

CALLS / EMAILS / TEXTS

LET'S REVIEW

○ FEEL ACCOMPLISHED?　　○ NOURISHED YOURSELF?　　○ PREPARE FOR TOMORROW?

WITH LOVE, *Emmelie*

NOTES AND REFLECTIONS

YOU GOT THIS!

REVENUE GOAL

PRIORITIES	INFLUENCE AND INCOME	**MINDSET MANTRA**
○		
○		
○		

MORNING

CALLS / EMAILS / TEXTS

AFTERNOON

EVENING

LET'S REVIEW

○ FEEL ACCOMPLISHED?   ○ NOURISHED YOURSELF?   ○ PREPARE FOR TOMORROW?

WITH LOVE, *Emmelie*

NOTES AND REFLECTIONS

YOU GOT THIS!

PRIORITIES	INFLUENCE AND INCOME	**MINDSET MANTRA**
○		
○		
○		

MORNING

AFTERNOON

EVENING

CALLS / EMAILS / TEXTS

LET'S REVIEW

○ FEEL ACCOMPLISHED?   ○ NOURISHED YOURSELF?   ○ PREPARE FOR TOMORROW?

WITH LOVE, *Emmelie*

NOTES AND REFLECTIONS

YOU GOT THIS!

REVENUE GOAL

PRIORITIES	INFLUENCE AND INCOME	**MINDSET MANTRA**
○		
○		
○		

MORNING

AFTERNOON

EVENING

CALLS / EMAILS / TEXTS

LET'S REVIEW

○ FEEL ACCOMPLISHED? ○ NOURISHED YOURSELF? ○ PREPARE FOR TOMORROW?

WITH LOVE, *Emmelie*

NOTES AND REFLECTIONS

YOU GOT THIS!

REVENUE GOAL

PRIORITIES	INFLUENCE AND INCOME	**MINDSET MANTRA**
○		
○		
○		

MORNING

AFTERNOON

EVENING

CALLS / EMAILS / TEXTS

LET'S REVIEW

◯ *FEEL ACCOMPLISHED?*   ◯ *NOURISHED YOURSELF?*   ◯ *PREPARE FOR TOMORROW?*

WITH LOVE, *Emmelie*

NOTES AND REFLECTIONS

YOU GOT THIS!

REVENUE GOAL

PRIORITIES	INFLUENCE AND INCOME	**MINDSET MANTRA**
○ ○ ○		

MORNING		CALLS / EMAILS / TEXTS

AFTERNOON

EVENING

LET'S REVIEW

◯ FEEL ACCOMPLISHED?   ◯ NOURISHED YOURSELF?   ◯ PREPARE FOR TOMORROW?

WITH LOVE, *Emmelie*

NOTES AND REFLECTIONS

YOU GOT THIS!

REVENUE GOAL

PRIORITIES	INFLUENCE AND INCOME	MINDSET MANTRA
○		
○		
○		

MORNING

AFTERNOON

EVENING

CALLS / EMAILS / TEXTS

LET'S REVIEW

○ FEEL ACCOMPLISHED?   ○ NOURISHED YOURSELF?   ○ PREPARE FOR TOMORROW?

WITH LOVE, *Emmelie*

NOTES AND REFLECTIONS

YOU GOT THIS!

REVENUE GOAL

PRIORITIES	INFLUENCE AND INCOME	**MINDSET MANTRA**
○		
○		
○		

MORNING	CALLS / EMAILS / TEXTS

AFTERNOON

EVENING

LET'S REVIEW

◯ FEEL ACCOMPLISHED?   ◯ NOURISHED YOURSELF?   ◯ PREPARE FOR TOMORROW?

WITH LOVE, *Emmelie*

NOTES AND REFLECTIONS

YOU GOT THIS!

REVENUE GOAL

PRIORITIES	INFLUENCE AND INCOME	**MINDSET MANTRA**
○		
○		
○		

MORNING

AFTERNOON

EVENING

CALLS / EMAILS / TEXTS

LET'S REVIEW

○ FEEL ACCOMPLISHED?   ○ NOURISHED YOURSELF?   ○ PREPARE FOR TOMORROW?

WITH LOVE, *Emmelie*

NOTES AND REFLECTIONS

NOTES AND REFLECTIONS

MONTH IN REVIEW

TRAFFIC	COMMUNITY	CONTENT
SESSIONS	TWITTER	BLOG POSTS
USERS	FACEBOOK	LEAD MAGNET
SALES	PINTEREST	EMAILS SENT
CONVERSION RATE	INSTAGRAM	WEBINARS
REFERRAL CHANNEL	LINKEDIN	PODCASTS
PRESS FEATURES	PERISCOPE	VIDEOS
	EMAIL SUBSCRIBERS	

WHAT KEPT ME MOTIVATED THIS MONTH?	WHAT COULD I HAVE DONE BETTER?

LESSONS	BEST OF THE BEST	MONEY MATTERS
O	MOST ENGAGING CHANNEL	REVENUE
	BEST SALES CHANNEL	MONEY SPENT
O	BEST CONTENT	PROFIT
	BEST SOCIAL POST	MOST POPULAR PRODUCT
O		

PRODUCT CREATION

PROBLEM

What is a problem that my audience is struggling with now?

AUDIENCE

Who has this problem?

PRODUCT

What will I create, repackage, or revamp to solve the problem.

PRODUCT TYPE
Book/eBook
Email Challenge
Online Course
Webinar
Product
Program
Other:

OUTLINE + CONTENT IDEAS

What is going in it? Think of this as the table of contents for your product.

SALES PAGE OUTLINE

HEADLINE

PROBLEM

PAIN POINT

OFFER

PRICING

TESTIMONIALS

ABOUT ME

QUALIFICATION

FREEBIE

FAQS

THE MONEY MAP

VALIDATION

Before I spend time and resources creating the thing I just outlined on the previous page, I will contact at least...

_____ *in the hope that* _____ *purchase by* _____
TARGETS   PRE-SALE CUSTOMERS   DEADLINE

Example: I will contact at least 100 people in the hope that 15 purchase by next Friday.

CONVERSIONS

Based on what happened during your pre-sale period, you can set goals for the real deal.

_____ *divided by* _____ *means I have a* _____
BUYERS   VISITORS   CONVERSION RATE

Example: 17 customers, out of the 75 people that saw the landing page means my conversion rate is: 22.6%

REVENUE

Now let's talk money.
How much do you want?

_____ *divided by* _____ *means I must sell* _____
MONTHLY GOALS   PRICE OF PRODUCT   SALES GOALS

Example: To make $5000 from a $39 product, I must sell 128 of them in a month.

TRAFFIC

With your revenue goal and your conversion rate, you can how much work is needed.

_____ *divided by* _____ *means I need* _____
SALES GOAL   CONVERSION RATE   LANDING PAGE VISITS

Example: To get 128 customers with a 22.6% conversion rate, I need to send 566 people to my landing page.

SOCIAL MEDIA PLAN

THINGS TO PROMOTE

TOPICS	SOCIAL POSTS	

NURTURE PLAN

FREEBIE

How can I begin to solve the problem for my audience without giving it all away?

TYPE
eBook
Challenge
Mini-Course
Webinar
Discount
Quiz
Other:

TRIPWIRE

What can I sell for under $30 that will further help my audience solve their problem?

BONUSES

What can I offer that will create a sense of urgency for my audience to buy within a specific timeframe?

DOWNSELL

What will be my last attempt to close the sale? What else can I offer to help solve their problem?

CONTENT IDEAS

EMAIL 1

Describe the problem then showcase the solution.

To Dos and Logistics

EMAIL 2

Share a way to solve the problem and present your product as a possble solution.

To Dos and Logistics

EMAIL 3

Invite them to purchase your offer and share the benefits.

To Dos and Logistics

EMAIL 4

Share a client/customer success story or your own personal success story.

To Dos and Logistics

EMAIL 5

Combat any rebuttals and answer any frequently asked questions.

To Dos and Logistics

EMAIL 6

Cart Closing Email

To Dos and Logistics

EMAIL 7

Last Chance Email

To Dos and Logistics

EMAIL 8

Downsell Email

To Dos and Logistics

THE MONTH'S MASTER PLAN

SUNDAY	MONDAY	TUESDAY	WEDNESDAY	THURSDAY	FRIDAY	SATURDAY

FREEBIE OUTLINE

PRODUCT TYPE
eBook
Email Challenge
Webinar
Coupon/Discount
Other:

TITLE

INTRO

PROBLEM

SOLUTION

OFFER

FREEBIE PAGE OUTLINE

HEADLINE

TEASER BULLETS AND DETAILS

FORM

CTA

TRIPWIRE OUTLINE

TITLE

PRODUCT TYPE

eBook	Whitepaper
Email Challenge	Report
Online Course	Coupon/Discount
Webinar	Other:

INTRO

PROBLEM

SOLUTION

OFFER

TRIPWIRE PAGE OUTLINE

THANK YOU

OFFER + DETAILS

SOCIAL PROOF

CTA

MASTER CHECKLIST

WEEK 1: THINGS TO WRITE
○ Social media schedule to drive traffic to free blog posts, lead magnet and offering sales page at least 20 days worth of promoting.
○ Free blog posts and/or podcast episodes
○ Lead magnet or freebie (ebook, email challenge, quiz, webinar, tutorial, checklist)
○ Lead magnet delivery email
○ Nurture sequence email funnel
○ Offering delivery sequence email
○ Sales page video
○ Create promo codes, countdowns, and landing pages for any bonuses

○ ### WEEK 2:THINGS TO DESIGN
○ Banner images for your landing pages
○ Cover graphic for your video
○ Mockups of your product, deliverables, or freebie
○ Flyer sharing your freebie
○ Blog post promotion graphics
○ Flyer for social media announcing the offering
○ Graphic with a testimonial on it
○ Flyer announcing the offering with the early bird price
○ Mockups of your product or deliverables from your service
○ Flash sale graphic
○ Instagram story/Snapchat/Pinterest versions of all of the above

WEEK 3: THINGS TO MAKE
○ Sales page
○ Lead magnet landing page
○ Lead magnet email sequence (delivery)
○ 3-5 email nurture funnel
○ Core offer sales page
○ Core offer email sequence (delivery + nurture funnel)
○ Webinar replay page
○ Create UTM tags for all links
○ Setup special promotions such as early bird prices or fast-action bonuses
○ Test all links, automations and email deliveries

WEEK 4: LAUNCH FLOW
○ Send an email to your current email list announcing the product or service.
○ Release a new blog post/video/podcast at least once a week during the promotion period.
○ Promote blog posts and freebie to capture emails and interest daily.
○ Potential customer downloads freebie and is added to an email list.
○ Potential customer receives email with freebie and email briefly mentions offering.
○ Potential customer is sent 3-7 emails promoting the product or service.
○ Customer that buys is removed from email list and added to an email list for the service.
○ Potential customer that hasn't purchase receives a flash sale or last chance email.
○ Update your funnel to make them evergreen, if needed.

AMPLIFICATION

INFLUENCERS	PARTNERS	PROMOTION/CAMPAIGN

AFFILIATES	SPONSORED/GUEST CONTENT

OTHER IDEAS

YOU GOT THIS!

REVENUE GOAL

PRIORITIES	INFLUENCE AND INCOME	**MINDSET MANTRA**
○		
○		
○		

MORNING

AFTERNOON

EVENING

CALLS / EMAILS / TEXTS

LET'S REVIEW

○ FEEL ACCOMPLISHED?   ○ NOURISHED YOURSELF?   ○ PREPARE FOR TOMORROW?

WITH LOVE, *Emmelie*

NOTES AND
REFLECTIONS

YOU GOT THIS!

PRIORITIES	INFLUENCE AND INCOME	**MINDSET MANTRA**
○		
○		
○		

MORNING

AFTERNOON

EVENING

CALLS / EMAILS / TEXTS

LET'S REVIEW

○ *FEEL ACCOMPLISHED?*   ○ *NOURISHED YOURSELF?*   ○ *PREPARE FOR TOMORROW?*

 WITH LOVE, *Emmelie*

NOTES AND REFLECTIONS

YOU GOT THIS!

REVENUE GOAL

PRIORITIES	INFLUENCE AND INCOME	**MINDSET MANTRA**
○		
○		
○		

MORNING

AFTERNOON

EVENING

CALLS / EMAILS / TEXTS

LET'S REVIEW

○ FEEL ACCOMPLISHED?   ○ NOURISHED YOURSELF?   ○ PREPARE FOR TOMORROW?

WITH LOVE, *Emmelie*

NOTES AND REFLECTIONS

YOU GOT THIS!

REVENUE GOAL

PRIORITIES	INFLUENCE AND INCOME	**MINDSET MANTRA**
○		
○		
○		

MORNING

AFTERNOON

EVENING

CALLS / EMAILS / TEXTS

LET'S REVIEW

◯ FEEL ACCOMPLISHED?   ◯ NOURISHED YOURSELF?   ◯ PREPARE FOR TOMORROW?

WITH LOVE, *Emmelie*

NOTES AND REFLECTIONS

YOU GOT THIS!

REVENUE GOAL

PRIORITIES	INFLUENCE AND INCOME	**MINDSET MANTRA**
○		
○		
○		

MORNING

AFTERNOON

EVENING

CALLS / EMAILS / TEXTS

LET'S REVIEW

○ FEEL ACCOMPLISHED?   ○ NOURISHED YOURSELF?   ○ PREPARE FOR TOMORROW?

WITH LOVE, *Emmelie*

NOTES AND REFLECTIONS

YOU GOT THIS!

REVENUE GOAL

PRIORITIES	INFLUENCE AND INCOME	**MINDSET MANTRA**
○		
○		
○		

MORNING

AFTERNOON

EVENING

CALLS / EMAILS / TEXTS

LET'S REVIEW

○ FEEL ACCOMPLISHED?   ○ NOURISHED YOURSELF?   ○ PREPARE FOR TOMORROW?

WITH LOVE, *Emmelie*

YOU GOT THIS!

REVENUE GOAL

PRIORITIES	INFLUENCE AND INCOME	**MINDSET MANTRA**
○		
○		
○		

MORNING

AFTERNOON

EVENING

CALLS / EMAILS / TEXTS

LET'S REVIEW

○ FEEL ACCOMPLISHED?   ○ NOURISHED YOURSELF?   ○ PREPARE FOR TOMORROW?

WITH LOVE, *Emmelie*

NOTES AND REFLECTIONS

YOU GOT THIS!

REVENUE GOAL

PRIORITIES	INFLUENCE AND INCOME	**MINDSET MANTRA**
○		
○		
○		

MORNING

AFTERNOON

EVENING

CALLS / EMAILS / TEXTS

LET'S REVIEW

◯ FEEL ACCOMPLISHED?   ◯ NOURISHED YOURSELF?   ◯ PREPARE FOR TOMORROW?

WITH LOVE, *Emmelie*

NOTES AND REFLECTIONS

YOU GOT THIS!

REVENUE GOAL

PRIORITIES	INFLUENCE AND INCOME	MINDSET MANTRA
○		
○		
○		

MORNING

AFTERNOON

EVENING

CALLS / EMAILS / TEXTS

LET'S REVIEW

○ FEEL ACCOMPLISHED?　　○ NOURISHED YOURSELF?　　○ PREPARE FOR TOMORROW?

WITH LOVE, *Emmelie*

NOTES AND
REFLECTIONS

YOU GOT THIS!

PRIORITIES	INFLUENCE AND INCOME	**MINDSET MANTRA**
○		
○		
○		

MORNING

AFTERNOON

EVENING

CALLS / EMAILS / TEXTS

LET'S REVIEW

◯ FEEL ACCOMPLISHED?   ◯ NOURISHED YOURSELF?   ◯ PREPARE FOR TOMORROW?

WITH LOVE, *Emmelie*

NOTES AND REFLECTIONS

YOU GOT THIS!

REVENUE GOAL

PRIORITIES	INFLUENCE AND INCOME	**MINDSET MANTRA**
○		
○		
○		

MORNING

AFTERNOON

EVENING

CALLS / EMAILS / TEXTS

LET'S REVIEW

 FEEL ACCOMPLISHED?   ⬭ NOURISHED YOURSELF?   ⬭ PREPARE FOR TOMORROW?

WITH LOVE, *Emmelie*

NOTES AND REFLECTIONS

YOU GOT THIS!

REVENUE GOAL

PRIORITIES	INFLUENCE AND INCOME	**MINDSET MANTRA**
○		
○		
○		

MORNING

AFTERNOON

EVENING

CALLS / EMAILS / TEXTS

LET'S REVIEW

 FEEL ACCOMPLISHED?   NOURISHED YOURSELF?   ◯ PREPARE FOR TOMORROW?

WITH LOVE, *Emmelie*

NOTES AND REFLECTIONS

YOU GOT THIS!

REVENUE GOAL

PRIORITIES	INFLUENCE AND INCOME	**MINDSET MANTRA**
○		
○		
○		

MORNING

AFTERNOON

EVENING

CALLS / EMAILS / TEXTS

LET'S REVIEW

○ FEEL ACCOMPLISHED?   ○ NOURISHED YOURSELF?   ○ PREPARE FOR TOMORROW?

WITH LOVE, *Emmelie*

NOTES AND REFLECTIONS

YOU GOT THIS!

REVENUE GOAL

PRIORITIES	INFLUENCE AND INCOME	**MINDSET MANTRA**
○		
○		
○		

MORNING

AFTERNOON

EVENING

CALLS / EMAILS / TEXTS

LET'S REVIEW

◯ FEEL ACCOMPLISHED?   ◯ NOURISHED YOURSELF?   ◯ PREPARE FOR TOMORROW?

WITH LOVE, *Emmelie*

YOU GOT THIS!

REVENUE GOAL

PRIORITIES	INFLUENCE AND INCOME	**MINDSET MANTRA**
○		
○		
○		

MORNING

AFTERNOON

EVENING

CALLS / EMAILS / TEXTS

LET'S REVIEW

○ FEEL ACCOMPLISHED?   ○ NOURISHED YOURSELF?   ○ PREPARE FOR TOMORROW?

WITH LOVE, *Emmelie*

YOU GOT THIS!

PRIORITIES	INFLUENCE AND INCOME	**MINDSET MANTRA**
○		
○		
○		

MORNING

AFTERNOON

EVENING

CALLS / EMAILS / TEXTS

LET'S REVIEW

○ *FEEL ACCOMPLISHED?*   ○ *NOURISHED YOURSELF?*   ○ *PREPARE FOR TOMORROW?*

WITH LOVE, *Emmelie*

NOTES AND REFLECTIONS

YOU GOT THIS!

PRIORITIES	INFLUENCE AND INCOME	**MINDSET MANTRA**
○		
○		
○		

MORNING

AFTERNOON

EVENING

CALLS / EMAILS / TEXTS

LET'S REVIEW

◯ FEEL ACCOMPLISHED?　　◯ NOURISHED YOURSELF?　　◯ PREPARE FOR TOMORROW?

WITH LOVE, *Emmelie*

NOTES AND REFLECTIONS

YOU GOT THIS!

REVENUE GOAL

PRIORITIES	INFLUENCE AND INCOME	**MINDSET MANTRA**
○		
○		
○		

MORNING

AFTERNOON

EVENING

CALLS / EMAILS / TEXTS

LET'S REVIEW

○ FEEL ACCOMPLISHED?   ○ NOURISHED YOURSELF?   ○ PREPARE FOR TOMORROW?

WITH LOVE, *Emmelie*

YOU GOT THIS!

REVENUE GOAL

PRIORITIES	INFLUENCE AND INCOME	**MINDSET MANTRA**
○		
○		
○		

MORNING

AFTERNOON

EVENING

CALLS / EMAILS / TEXTS

LET'S REVIEW

◯ FEEL ACCOMPLISHED? ◯ NOURISHED YOURSELF? ◯ PREPARE FOR TOMORROW?

WITH LOVE, *Emmelie*

NOTES AND REFLECTIONS

YOU GOT THIS!

REVENUE GOAL

PRIORITIES	INFLUENCE AND INCOME	**MINDSET MANTRA**
○		
○		
○		

MORNING

AFTERNOON

EVENING

CALLS / EMAILS / TEXTS

LET'S REVIEW

○ FEEL ACCOMPLISHED?   ○ NOURISHED YOURSELF?   ○ PREPARE FOR TOMORROW?

WITH LOVE, *Emmelie*

YOU GOT THIS!

REVENUE GOAL

PRIORITIES	INFLUENCE AND INCOME	**MINDSET MANTRA**
○		
○		
○		

MORNING

AFTERNOON

EVENING

CALLS / EMAILS / TEXTS

LET'S REVIEW

○ FEEL ACCOMPLISHED?   ○ NOURISHED YOURSELF?   ○ PREPARE FOR TOMORROW?

WITH LOVE, *Emmelie*

NOTES AND REFLECTIONS

YOU GOT THIS!

REVENUE GOAL

PRIORITIES	INFLUENCE AND INCOME	**MINDSET MANTRA**
○		
○		
○		

MORNING

AFTERNOON

EVENING

CALLS / EMAILS / TEXTS

LET'S REVIEW

○ FEEL ACCOMPLISHED?   ○ NOURISHED YOURSELF?   ○ PREPARE FOR TOMORROW?

WITH LOVE, *Emmelie*

YOU GOT THIS!

REVENUE GOAL

PRIORITIES	INFLUENCE AND INCOME	**MINDSET MANTRA**
○		
○		
○		

MORNING

AFTERNOON

EVENING

CALLS / EMAILS / TEXTS

LET'S REVIEW

○ FEEL ACCOMPLISHED?   ○ NOURISHED YOURSELF?   ○ PREPARE FOR TOMORROW?

WITH LOVE, *Emmelie*

NOTES AND REFLECTIONS

YOU GOT THIS!

REVENUE GOAL

PRIORITIES	INFLUENCE AND INCOME	**MINDSET MANTRA**
○		
○		
○		

MORNING

AFTERNOON

EVENING

CALLS / EMAILS / TEXTS

LET'S REVIEW

◯ FEEL ACCOMPLISHED?   ◯ NOURISHED YOURSELF?   ◯ PREPARE FOR TOMORROW?

WITH LOVE, *Emmelie*

NOTES AND REFLECTIONS

YOU GOT THIS!

REVENUE GOAL

PRIORITIES	INFLUENCE AND INCOME	**MINDSET MANTRA**
○		
○		
○		

MORNING

AFTERNOON

EVENING

CALLS / EMAILS / TEXTS

LET'S REVIEW

 FEEL ACCOMPLISHED?   NOURISHED YOURSELF?   ○ PREPARE FOR TOMORROW?

WITH LOVE, *Emmelie*

NOTES AND REFLECTIONS

YOU GOT THIS!

REVENUE GOAL

PRIORITIES	INFLUENCE AND INCOME	**MINDSET MANTRA**
○		
○		
○		

MORNING

AFTERNOON

EVENING

CALLS / EMAILS / TEXTS

LET'S REVIEW

 FEEL ACCOMPLISHED?   ◯ NOURISHED YOURSELF?   ◯ PREPARE FOR TOMORROW?

WITH LOVE, *Emmelie*

YOU GOT THIS!

REVENUE GOAL

PRIORITIES	INFLUENCE AND INCOME	**MINDSET MANTRA**
○		
○		
○		

MORNING

AFTERNOON

EVENING

CALLS / EMAILS / TEXTS

LET'S REVIEW

◯ FEEL ACCOMPLISHED?   ◯ NOURISHED YOURSELF?   ◯ PREPARE FOR TOMORROW?

WITH LOVE, *Emmelie*

NOTES AND REFLECTIONS

YOU GOT THIS!

REVENUE GOAL

PRIORITIES	INFLUENCE AND INCOME	**MINDSET MANTRA**
○		
○		
○		

MORNING

AFTERNOON

EVENING

CALLS / EMAILS / TEXTS

LET'S REVIEW

◯ FEEL ACCOMPLISHED?   ◯ NOURISHED YOURSELF?   ◯ PREPARE FOR TOMORROW?

WITH LOVE, *Emmelie*

NOTES AND REFLECTIONS

YOU GOT THIS!

REVENUE GOAL

PRIORITIES	INFLUENCE AND INCOME	**MINDSET MANTRA**
○		
○		
○		

MORNING

AFTERNOON

EVENING

CALLS / EMAILS / TEXTS

LET'S REVIEW

◯ FEEL ACCOMPLISHED? ◯ NOURISHED YOURSELF? ◯ PREPARE FOR TOMORROW?

WITH LOVE, *Emmelie*

YOU GOT THIS!

REVENUE GOAL

PRIORITIES	INFLUENCE AND INCOME	**MINDSET MANTRA**
○		
○		
○		

MORNING	CALLS / EMAILS / TEXTS

AFTERNOON

EVENING

LET'S REVIEW

◯ FEEL ACCOMPLISHED?   ◯ NOURISHED YOURSELF?   ◯ PREPARE FOR TOMORROW?

WITH LOVE, *Emmelie*

NOTES AND REFLECTIONS

YOU GOT THIS!

PRIORITIES	INFLUENCE AND INCOME	**MINDSET MANTRA**
○		
○		
○		

MORNING

AFTERNOON

EVENING

CALLS / EMAILS / TEXTS

LET'S REVIEW

○ FEEL ACCOMPLISHED? ○ NOURISHED YOURSELF? ○ PREPARE FOR TOMORROW?

WITH LOVE, *Emmelie*

NOTES AND REFLECTIONS

NOTES AND REFLECTIONS

MONTH IN REVIEW

TRAFFIC	COMMUNITY	CONTENT
SESSIONS	TWITTER	BLOG POSTS
USERS	FACEBOOK	LEAD MAGNET
SALES	PINTEREST	EMAILS SENT
CONVERSION RATE	INSTAGRAM	WEBINARS
REFERRAL CHANNEL	LINKEDIN	PODCASTS
PRESS FEATURES	PERISCOPE	VIDEOS
	EMAIL SUBSCRIBERS	

WHAT KEPT ME MOTIVATED THIS MONTH?	WHAT COULD I HAVE DONE BETTER?

LESSONS	BEST OF THE BEST	MONEY MATTERS
O	MOST ENGAGING CHANNEL	REVENUE
	BEST SALES CHANNEL	MONEY SPENT
O	BEST CONTENT	PROFIT
	BEST SOCIAL POST	MOST POPULAR PRODUCT
O		

PRODUCT CREATION

PROBLEM

What is a problem that my audience is struggling with now?

AUDIENCE

Who has this problem?

PRODUCT

What will I create, repackage, or revamp to solve the problem.

PRODUCT TYPE
Book/eBook
Email Challenge
Online Course
Webinar
Product
Program
Other:

OUTLINE + CONTENT IDEAS

What is going in it? Think of this as the table of contents for your product.

SALES PAGE OUTLINE

HEADLINE

PROBLEM

PAIN POINT

OFFER

PRICING

TESTIMONIALS

ABOUT ME

QUALIFICATION

FREEBIE

FAQS

THE MONEY MAP

VALIDATION

Before I spend time and resources creating the thing I just outlined on the previous page, I will contact at least...

_____ *in the hope that* _____ *purchase by* _____
TARGETS   PRE-SALE CUSTOMERS   DEADLINE

Example: I will contact at least 100 people in the hope that 15 purchase by next Friday.

CONVERSIONS

Based on what happened during your pre-sale period, you can set goals for the real deal.

_____ *divided by* _____ *means I have a* _____
BUYERS   VISITORS   CONVERSION RATE

Example: 17 customers, out of the 75 people that saw the landing page means my conversion rate is: 22.6%

REVENUE

Now let's talk money.
How much do you want?

_____ *divided by* _____ *means I must sell* _____
MONTHLY GOALS   PRICE OF PRODUCT   SALES GOALS

Example: To make $5000 from a $39 product, I must sell 128 of them in a month.

TRAFFIC

With your revenue goal and your conversion rate, you can how much work is needed.

_____ *divided by* _____ *means I need* _____
SALES GOAL   CONVERSION RATE   LANDING PAGE VISITS

Example: To get 128 customers with a 22.6% conversion rate, I need to send 566 people to my landing page.

SOCIAL MEDIA PLAN

THINGS TO PROMOTE

TOPICS	SOCIAL POSTS	

NURTURE PLAN

FREEBIE

How can I begin to solve the problem for my audience without giving it all away?

TYPE
eBook
Challenge
Mini-Course
Webinar
Discount
Quiz
Other:

TRIPWIRE

What can I sell for under $30 that will further help my audience solve their problem?

BONUSES

What can I offer that will create a sense of urgency for my audience to buy within a specific timeframe?

DOWNSELL

What will be my last attempt to close the sale? What else can I offer to help solve their problem?

CONTENT IDEAS

EMAIL 1

Describe the problem then showcase the solution.

To Dos and Logistics

EMAIL 2

Share a way to solve the problem and present your product as a possble solution.

To Dos and Logistics

EMAIL 3

Invite them to purchase your offer and share the benefits.

To Dos and Logistics

EMAIL 4

Share a client/customer success story or your own personal success story.

To Dos and Logistics

EMAIL 5

Combat any rebuttals and answer any frequently asked questions.

To Dos and Logistics

EMAIL 6

Cart Closing Email

To Dos and Logistics

EMAIL 7

Last Chance Email

To Dos and Logistics

EMAIL 8

Downsell Email

To Dos and Logistics

THE MONTH'S MASTER PLAN

SUNDAY	MONDAY	TUESDAY	WEDNESDAY	THURSDAY	FRIDAY	SATURDAY

FREEBIE OUTLINE

PRODUCT TYPE
eBook
Email Challenge
Webinar
Coupon/Discount
Other:

TITLE

INTRO

PROBLEM

SOLUTION

OFFER

FREEBIE PAGE OUTLINE

HEADLINE

TEASER BULLETS AND DETAILS

FORM

CTA

TRIPWIRE OUTLINE

TITLE

PRODUCT TYPE

eBook	Whitepaper
Email Challenge	Report
Online Course	Coupon/Discount
Webinar	Other:

INTRO

PROBLEM

SOLUTION

OFFER

TRIPWIRE PAGE OUTLINE

THANK YOU

OFFER + DETAILS

SOCIAL PROOF

CTA

MASTER CHECKLIST

WEEK 1: THINGS TO WRITE
○ Social media schedule to drive traffic to free blog posts, lead magnet and offering sales page at least 20 days worth of promoting.
○ Free blog posts and/or podcast episodes
○ Lead magnet or freebie (ebook, email challenge, quiz, webinar, tutorial, checklist)
○ Lead magnet delivery email
○ Nurture sequence email funnel
○ Offering delivery sequence email
○ Sales page video
○ Create promo codes, countdowns, and landing pages for any bonuses

○ WEEK 2:THINGS TO DESIGN
○ Banner images for your landing pages
○ Cover graphic for your video
○ Mockups of your product, deliverables, or freebie
○ Flyer sharing your freebie
○ Blog post promotion graphics
○ Flyer for social media announcing the offering
○ Graphic with a testimonial on it
○ Flyer announcing the offering with the early bird price
○ Mockups of your product or deliverables from your service
○ Flash sale graphic
○ Instagram story/Snapchat/Pinterest versions of all of the above

WEEK 3: THINGS TO MAKE
○ Sales page
○ Lead magnet landing page
○ Lead magnet email sequence (delivery)
○ 3-5 email nurture funnel
○ Core offer sales page
○ Core offer email sequence (delivery + nurture funnel)
○ Webinar replay page
○ Create UTM tags for all links
○ Setup special promotions such as early bird prices or fast-action bonuses
○ Test all links, automations and email deliveries

WEEK 4: LAUNCH FLOW
○ Send an email to your current email list announcing the product or service.
○ Release a new blog post/video/podcast at least once a week during the promotion period.
○ Promote blog posts and freebie to capture emails and interest daily.
○ Potential customer downloads freebie and is added to an email list.
○ Potential customer receives email with freebie and email briefly mentions offering.
○ Potential customer is sent 3-7 emails promoting the product or service.
○ Customer that buys is removed from email list and added to an email list for the service.
○ Potential customer that hasn't purchase receives a flash sale or last chance email.
○ Update your funnel to make them evergreen, if needed.

AMPLIFICATION

INFLUENCERS	PARTNERS	PROMOTION/CAMPAIGN

AFFILIATES	SPONSORED/GUEST CONTENT

OTHER IDEAS

YOU GOT THIS!

REVENUE GOAL

PRIORITIES	INFLUENCE AND INCOME	**MINDSET MANTRA**
○		
○		
○		

MORNING

AFTERNOON

EVENING

CALLS / EMAILS / TEXTS

LET'S REVIEW

○ FEEL ACCOMPLISHED?　　○ NOURISHED YOURSELF?　　○ PREPARE FOR TOMORROW?

WITH LOVE, *Emmelie*

NOTES AND REFLECTIONS

YOU GOT THIS!

REVENUE GOAL

PRIORITIES	INFLUENCE AND INCOME	**MINDSET MANTRA**
○		
○		
○		

MORNING

AFTERNOON

EVENING

CALLS / EMAILS / TEXTS

LET'S REVIEW

○ FEEL ACCOMPLISHED?   ○ NOURISHED YOURSELF?   ○ PREPARE FOR TOMORROW?

WITH LOVE, *Emmelie*

NOTES AND REFLECTIONS

YOU GOT THIS!

PRIORITIES	INFLUENCE AND INCOME	MINDSET MANTRA
○		
○		
○		

MORNING

AFTERNOON

EVENING

CALLS / EMAILS / TEXTS

LET'S REVIEW

 FEEL ACCOMPLISHED?   *NOURISHED YOURSELF?*   ( ) *PREPARE FOR TOMORROW?*

WITH LOVE, *Emmelie*

NOTES AND REFLECTIONS

YOU GOT THIS!

REVENUE GOAL

PRIORITIES	INFLUENCE AND INCOME	**MINDSET MANTRA**
○		
○		
○		

MORNING

AFTERNOON

EVENING

CALLS / EMAILS / TEXTS

LET'S REVIEW

○ FEEL ACCOMPLISHED?   ○ NOURISHED YOURSELF?   ○ PREPARE FOR TOMORROW?

WITH LOVE, *Emmelie*

NOTES AND REFLECTIONS

YOU GOT THIS!

REVENUE GOAL

PRIORITIES	INFLUENCE AND INCOME	**MINDSET MANTRA**
○		
○		
○		

MORNING

AFTERNOON

EVENING

CALLS / EMAILS / TEXTS

LET'S REVIEW

○ FEEL ACCOMPLISHED? ○ NOURISHED YOURSELF? ○ PREPARE FOR TOMORROW?

WITH LOVE, *Emmelie*

NOTES AND REFLECTIONS

YOU GOT THIS!

REVENUE GOAL

PRIORITIES	INFLUENCE AND INCOME	**MINDSET MANTRA**
○		
○		
○		

MORNING

AFTERNOON

EVENING

CALLS / EMAILS / TEXTS

LET'S REVIEW

○ FEEL ACCOMPLISHED?   ○ NOURISHED YOURSELF?   ○ PREPARE FOR TOMORROW?

WITH LOVE, *Emmelie*

NOTES AND REFLECTIONS

YOU GOT THIS!

REVENUE GOAL

PRIORITIES	INFLUENCE AND INCOME	**MINDSET MANTRA**
○		
○		
○		

MORNING

AFTERNOON

EVENING

CALLS / EMAILS / TEXTS

LET'S REVIEW

◯ FEEL ACCOMPLISHED?   ◯ NOURISHED YOURSELF?   ◯ PREPARE FOR TOMORROW?

WITH LOVE, *Emmelie*

NOTES AND REFLECTIONS

YOU GOT THIS!

REVENUE GOAL

PRIORITIES	INFLUENCE AND INCOME	**MINDSET MANTRA**
○		
○		
○		

MORNING

AFTERNOON

EVENING

CALLS / EMAILS / TEXTS

LET'S REVIEW

○ FEEL ACCOMPLISHED?　　○ NOURISHED YOURSELF?　　○ PREPARE FOR TOMORROW?

WITH LOVE, *Emmelie*

NOTES AND REFLECTIONS

YOU GOT THIS!

REVENUE GOAL

PRIORITIES	INFLUENCE AND INCOME	**MINDSET MANTRA**
○ ○ ○		

MORNING

AFTERNOON

EVENING

CALLS / EMAILS / TEXTS

LET'S REVIEW

○ FEEL ACCOMPLISHED?　　○ NOURISHED YOURSELF?　　○ PREPARE FOR TOMORROW?

WITH LOVE, *Emmelie*

NOTES AND REFLECTIONS

YOU GOT THIS!

PRIORITIES	INFLUENCE AND INCOME	**MINDSET MANTRA**
○		
○		
○		

MORNING

AFTERNOON

EVENING

CALLS / EMAILS / TEXTS

LET'S REVIEW

○ FEEL ACCOMPLISHED? ○ NOURISHED YOURSELF? ○ PREPARE FOR TOMORROW?

WITH LOVE, *Emmelie*

NOTES AND REFLECTIONS

YOU GOT THIS!

REVENUE GOAL

PRIORITIES	INFLUENCE AND INCOME	**MINDSET MANTRA**
○		
○		
○		

MORNING

AFTERNOON

EVENING

CALLS / EMAILS / TEXTS

LET'S REVIEW

○ FEEL ACCOMPLISHED?   ○ NOURISHED YOURSELF?   ○ PREPARE FOR TOMORROW?

WITH LOVE, *Emmelie*

NOTES AND REFLECTIONS

YOU GOT THIS!

REVENUE GOAL

PRIORITIES	INFLUENCE AND INCOME	**MINDSET MANTRA**
○		
○		
○		

MORNING

AFTERNOON

EVENING

CALLS / EMAILS / TEXTS

LET'S REVIEW

○ FEEL ACCOMPLISHED?   ○ NOURISHED YOURSELF?   ○ PREPARE FOR TOMORROW?

WITH LOVE, *Emmelie*

NOTES AND REFLECTIONS

YOU GOT THIS!

REVENUE GOAL

PRIORITIES	INFLUENCE AND INCOME	**MINDSET MANTRA**
○		
○		
○		

MORNING

AFTERNOON

EVENING

CALLS / EMAILS / TEXTS

LET'S REVIEW

○ FEEL ACCOMPLISHED?   ○ NOURISHED YOURSELF?   ○ PREPARE FOR TOMORROW?

WITH LOVE, *Emmelie*

YOU GOT THIS!

PRIORITIES	INFLUENCE AND INCOME	**MINDSET MANTRA**
○		
○		
○		

MORNING

AFTERNOON

EVENING

CALLS / EMAILS / TEXTS

LET'S REVIEW

○ FEEL ACCOMPLISHED?   ○ NOURISHED YOURSELF?   ○ PREPARE FOR TOMORROW?

WITH LOVE, *Emmelie*

NOTES AND REFLECTIONS

YOU GOT THIS!

REVENUE GOAL

PRIORITIES	INFLUENCE AND INCOME	**MINDSET MANTRA**
○		
○		
○		

MORNING

AFTERNOON

EVENING

CALLS / EMAILS / TEXTS

LET'S REVIEW

○ FEEL ACCOMPLISHED?　　○ NOURISHED YOURSELF?　　○ PREPARE FOR TOMORROW?

WITH LOVE, *Emmelie*

NOTES AND REFLECTIONS

YOU GOT THIS!

REVENUE GOAL

PRIORITIES	INFLUENCE AND INCOME	**MINDSET MANTRA**
○		
○		
○		

MORNING

AFTERNOON

EVENING

CALLS / EMAILS / TEXTS

LET'S REVIEW

○ FEEL ACCOMPLISHED?   ○ NOURISHED YOURSELF?   ○ PREPARE FOR TOMORROW?

WITH LOVE, *Emmelie*

NOTES AND REFLECTIONS

YOU GOT THIS!

REVENUE GOAL

PRIORITIES	INFLUENCE AND INCOME	**MINDSET MANTRA**
○		
○		
○		

MORNING

AFTERNOON

EVENING

CALLS / EMAILS / TEXTS

LET'S REVIEW

○ FEEL ACCOMPLISHED? ○ NOURISHED YOURSELF? ○ PREPARE FOR TOMORROW?

WITH LOVE, *Emmelie*

NOTES AND
REFLECTIONS

YOU GOT THIS!

REVENUE GOAL

PRIORITIES	INFLUENCE AND INCOME	**MINDSET MANTRA**
○		
○		
○		

MORNING

AFTERNOON

EVENING

CALLS / EMAILS / TEXTS

LET'S REVIEW

○ FEEL ACCOMPLISHED?   ○ NOURISHED YOURSELF?   ○ PREPARE FOR TOMORROW?

WITH LOVE, *Emmelie*

NOTES AND REFLECTIONS

YOU GOT THIS!

REVENUE GOAL

PRIORITIES	INFLUENCE AND INCOME	**MINDSET MANTRA**
○		
○		
○		

MORNING

AFTERNOON

EVENING

CALLS / EMAILS / TEXTS

LET'S REVIEW

○ FEEL ACCOMPLISHED?   ○ NOURISHED YOURSELF?   ○ PREPARE FOR TOMORROW?

WITH LOVE, *Emmelie*

NOTES AND REFLECTIONS

YOU GOT THIS!

REVENUE GOAL

PRIORITIES	INFLUENCE AND INCOME	**MINDSET MANTRA**
○		
○		
○		

MORNING

AFTERNOON

EVENING

CALLS / EMAILS / TEXTS

LET'S REVIEW

○ FEEL ACCOMPLISHED?　　○ NOURISHED YOURSELF?　　○ PREPARE FOR TOMORROW?

WITH LOVE, *Emmelie*

NOTES AND REFLECTIONS

YOU GOT THIS!

REVENUE GOAL

PRIORITIES	INFLUENCE AND INCOME	**MINDSET MANTRA**
○		
○		
○		

MORNING	CALLS / EMAILS / TEXTS

AFTERNOON

EVENING

LET'S REVIEW

 FEEL ACCOMPLISHED?   NOURISHED YOURSELF?   ◯ PREPARE FOR TOMORROW?

WITH LOVE, *Emmelie*

NOTES AND REFLECTIONS

YOU GOT THIS!

REVENUE GOAL

PRIORITIES	INFLUENCE AND INCOME	**MINDSET MANTRA**
○		
○		
○		

MORNING	CALLS / EMAILS / TEXTS

AFTERNOON

EVENING

LET'S REVIEW

◯ FEEL ACCOMPLISHED?   ◯ NOURISHED YOURSELF?   ◯ PREPARE FOR TOMORROW?

WITH LOVE, *Emmelie*

NOTES AND REFLECTIONS

YOU GOT THIS!

REVENUE GOAL

PRIORITIES	INFLUENCE AND INCOME	**MINDSET MANTRA**
○		
○		
○		

MORNING

AFTERNOON

EVENING

CALLS / EMAILS / TEXTS

LET'S REVIEW

◯ FEEL ACCOMPLISHED?   ◯ NOURISHED YOURSELF?   ◯ PREPARE FOR TOMORROW?

WITH LOVE, *Emmelie*

NOTES AND REFLECTIONS

YOU GOT THIS!

REVENUE GOAL

PRIORITIES	INFLUENCE AND INCOME	**MINDSET MANTRA**
○		
○		
○		

MORNING

AFTERNOON

EVENING

CALLS / EMAILS / TEXTS

LET'S REVIEW

○ FEEL ACCOMPLISHED?   ○ NOURISHED YOURSELF?   ○ PREPARE FOR TOMORROW?

WITH LOVE, *Emmelie*

NOTES AND
REFLECTIONS

YOU GOT THIS!

REVENUE GOAL

PRIORITIES	INFLUENCE AND INCOME	**MINDSET MANTRA**
○		
○		
○		

MORNING	CALLS / EMAILS / TEXTS

AFTERNOON

EVENING

LET'S REVIEW

◯ FEEL ACCOMPLISHED?   ◯ NOURISHED YOURSELF?   ◯ PREPARE FOR TOMORROW?

WITH LOVE, *Emmelie*

NOTES AND REFLECTIONS

YOU GOT THIS!

REVENUE GOAL

PRIORITIES	INFLUENCE AND INCOME	**MINDSET MANTRA**
○		
○		
○		

MORNING

AFTERNOON

EVENING

CALLS / EMAILS / TEXTS

LET'S REVIEW

○ FEEL ACCOMPLISHED?   ○ NOURISHED YOURSELF?   ○ PREPARE FOR TOMORROW?

WITH LOVE, *Emmelie*

NOTES AND REFLECTIONS

YOU GOT THIS!

REVENUE GOAL

PRIORITIES	INFLUENCE AND INCOME	**MINDSET MANTRA**
○		
○		
○		

MORNING

AFTERNOON

EVENING

CALLS / EMAILS / TEXTS

LET'S REVIEW

○ FEEL ACCOMPLISHED? ○ NOURISHED YOURSELF? ○ PREPARE FOR TOMORROW?

WITH LOVE, *Emmelie*

**NOTES AND
REFLECTIONS**

YOU GOT THIS!

PRIORITIES	INFLUENCE AND INCOME	**MINDSET MANTRA**
O		
O		
O		

MORNING	CALLS / EMAILS / TEXTS

AFTERNOON

EVENING

LET'S REVIEW

◯ *FEEL ACCOMPLISHED?*   ◯ *NOURISHED YOURSELF?*   ◯ *PREPARE FOR TOMORROW?*

WITH LOVE, *Emmelie*

YOU GOT THIS!

REVENUE GOAL

PRIORITIES	INFLUENCE AND INCOME	**MINDSET MANTRA**
○		
○		
○		

MORNING

AFTERNOON

EVENING

CALLS / EMAILS / TEXTS

LET'S REVIEW

◯ FEEL ACCOMPLISHED?   ◯ NOURISHED YOURSELF?   ◯ PREPARE FOR TOMORROW?

WITH LOVE, *Emmelie*

NOTES AND REFLECTIONS

YOU GOT THIS!

PRIORITIES	INFLUENCE AND INCOME	MINDSET MANTRA
○		
○		
○		

MORNING

AFTERNOON

EVENING

CALLS / EMAILS / TEXTS

LET'S REVIEW

○ FEEL ACCOMPLISHED?   ○ NOURISHED YOURSELF?   ○ PREPARE FOR TOMORROW?

WITH LOVE, *Emmelie*

YOU GOT THIS!

REVENUE GOAL

PRIORITIES	INFLUENCE AND INCOME	**MINDSET MANTRA**
○		
○		
○		

MORNING

AFTERNOON

EVENING

CALLS / EMAILS / TEXTS

LET'S REVIEW

 FEEL ACCOMPLISHED?   NOURISHED YOURSELF?   ◯ PREPARE FOR TOMORROW?

WITH LOVE, *Emmelie*

NOTES AND REFLECTIONS

MONTH IN REVIEW

TRAFFIC	COMMUNITY	CONTENT
SESSIONS	TWITTER	BLOG POSTS
USERS	FACEBOOK	LEAD MAGNET
SALES	PINTEREST	EMAILS SENT
CONVERSION RATE	INSTAGRAM	WEBINARS
REFERRAL CHANNEL	LINKEDIN	PODCASTS
PRESS FEATURES	PERISCOPE	VIDEOS
	EMAIL SUBSCRIBERS	

WHAT KEPT ME MOTIVATED THIS MONTH?	WHAT COULD I HAVE DONE BETTER?

LESSONS	BEST OF THE BEST	MONEY MATTERS
O	MOST ENGAGING CHANNEL	REVENUE
	BEST SALES CHANNEL	MONEY SPENT
O	BEST CONTENT	PROFIT
	BEST SOCIAL POST	MOST POPULAR PRODUCT
O		

Made in the USA
Middletown, DE
11 April 2018